30 DAYS TO VIRTUAL PRODUCTIVITY SUCCESS

30 DAYS TO VIRTUAL PRODUCTIVITY SUCCESS

The 30-Day Results Guide to Making the Most of Your Time, Expanding Your Contacts, and Growing Your Business

By Gail Z. Martin

CAREER PRESS

Pompton Plains, NJ

30 Days to Virtual Productivity Success
Edited and Typeset by Diana Ghazzawi
Cover design by Jeff Piasky
Printed in the U.S.A.

To order this title, please call toll-free 1-800-CAREER-1 (NJ and Canada: 201-848-0310) to order using VISA or MasterCard, or for further information on books from Career Press.

The Career Press, Inc.
220 West Parkway, Unit 12
Pompton Plains, NJ 07444
www.careerpress.com

Library of Congress Cataloging-in-Publication Data
Martin, Gail Z., 1962-
    30 days to virtual productivity success : the 30-day results guide to making the most of your time, expanding your contacts, and growing your business / by Gail Z. Martin.
        p. cm.
    Includes index.
        ISBN 978-1-60163-226-5 -- ISBN 978-1-60163-581-5 (ebook)
    1. Internet marketing. 2. Small business--Growth. 3. Business planning. 4. Time management. 5. Information technology--Management. I. Title. II. Title: Thirty days to virtual productivity success.

HF5415.1265.M3293 2012
658.5'15--dc23

                                                           2012013337

Contents

Author's Note

publisher for the performance, effectiveness, or applicability of any Websites listed or linked to in this book. The Websites cited in the book and all associated trademarks are the property of their rightful owners. Neither the author nor the publisher control the content on any third-party Websites mentioned in the book, and no warranty or guarantee of results is made regarding the products or services offered by third-party sites mentioned in the book. All brand names are the property of their rightful owners.

~~~

A word about the way this book works. If you read *30 Days to Social Media Success* or other books in this series, you may find the first seven chapters to be familiar. That's because they lay the groundwork for the rest of the advice in the book. If you're a new reader, these chapters are essential to get the maximum value from the book. If you're a returning reader, feel free to review these chapters so that the information is fresh in your mind; you'll need it going forward.

Introduction

The Internet has changed the way we understand productivity. If you can remember a time before Google, YouTube, and Amazon, then you may remember needing to trek to a library to find information, open a phone book to find contact data, and travel to a real store (or use a catalog) to buy anything.

Times have changed.

The downside of being able to access the world at the click of a mouse is that we often extend the expectation for immediate results to the rest of our lives. Computers, the Internet, and mobile apps have led to tremendous time savings and undoubtedly contributed to gains in productivity. But the other part of the equation—business development, expanding your contacts, and growing your business—require equal parts tech savvy and old-fashioned patience and people skills.

This book attempts to bridge the divide between sheer computer (or mobile) processing power and the outcomes you desire: less wasted time, more productive personal business connections, and ultimately, more business growth. Some of the tips deal with programs and apps which you may have not yet discovered, but which can make your time more productive. But some of the most important information in the book focuses on the strategy behind the actions, a mind shift that is necessary to get the most out of the gadgets that surround us.

Real productivity, as well as successful business development, begins with a plan and a clear understanding of the intended audience. It's an interesting paradox that although today's technology now makes it easy for us to reach millions of people with our messages, real results spring from focusing only on those ideal customers who are going to be most receptive—and most likely to buy.

In this book, I'll be using the term "business development" to encompass the collective gains from enhanced productivity and effective networking that produce growth. There are other factors that can also contribute to growth, including the savvy use of social media along with online PR and marketing (which I cover in two separate books). For now, we'll focus on taking a strategic, action-oriented approach to boosting productivity and increasing networking effectiveness, while not losing touch with the human connections that are at the true heart of growth.

The first seven chapters provide the foundation for the strategy that will carry you through the rest of the book. These chapters help you focus on your strategy, goals, and audience to get the most out of the tips, tricks, and techniques presented later in the book. Without a solid foundation, the tools won't be as effective, so I highly recommend taking the time to read (and think through) the first seven chapters first.

Navigating this new online world requires taking risks, being open to innovation, and having a clear understanding that this is uncharted territory. Welcome to the frontier, where fortunes are made and lost, and anything is possible.

1
Why Most Business Development Efforts Fail

Networking and business development horror stories. You've probably heard them. You may have one yourself. These are the stories about how someone tried a new technique, sent out a press release, or made an effort to grow their business, and "it didn't work."

I've heard plenty of these stories. And as with most urban legends, there's usually more to the story than meets the eye. If you're reading this book, you're a coach, consultant, speaker, author, or owner of a small business, and you want more from your business development efforts than you're currently getting. You may not be investing in ways to increase productivity and expand your network at all because your business is new, or because you're afraid to fail. Or it may be that your business development efforts are chugging along with mediocre returns or muddled measurement.

Take heart. Growing your business isn't mysterious, and once you understand how the pieces fit together, you'll be in a better position to manage growth for your own company or to oversee someone to handle it for you. Let's start by looking at the seven most common reasons that business development plans fail.

1. No planning. This is true in both large and small businesses. Many business development efforts fail because there is no link between the business development actions and the bottom-line business plan goals that drive revenue. This happens because decision makers get caught up with a vivid, creative idea that isn't accountable to the bottom line, or because they forget the human side of the equation. Business development without a plan is a disaster waiting to happen.

2. Inappropriate actions. If there is no plan, then business development actions may conflict with each other. It's unlikely that scattershot actions will support a business plan goal. Disappointing results come about because of a "ready, fire, aim" approach in which actions aren't anchored to business objectives and target audiences. Attempts to copy what a successful competitor is doing without understanding why (or whether) the action is working for them is also a dangerous approach.

3. Lack of clarity about the target market. Mass marketing is dead (and highly unproductive). Trying to establish too broad a personal network without a clear target is wasteful and unsuccessful. You can't hit a target if you haven't identified it. There is a sweet spot of potential customers who could become your ideal clients. You'll need to get to know them to win them.

4. Lack of clear goals. If you don't have an upfront understanding of what success will look like, you won't know when you achieve it. Not only do your business development actions need to be linked to specific business goals, but each action should be measurable. Build in measurability up front so expectations are clear.

5. Unreasonable expectations. Just increasing productivity isn't likely to create a big spike in sales. Just joining a

new networking organization probably won't save your company. Many people become disillusioned with business development because they don't understand the benchmarks for successful programs. For example, most direct-mail professionals are thrilled to get a 1-percent response rate. One percent! Yet many small businesses send out a postcard mailing and quit in disgust, expecting a response of 20 percent, 30 percent, or more. Many people give up on networking efforts after a few weeks, not realizing that it can take months, even years, to build trust and establish strong relationships that lead to sales. It's important to have realistic expectations so you recognize success when you see it.

6. Lack of clarity on how business development works. For many people, business development is a lot like a DVD player. They don't know (and don't care) how it works. Your odds of creating successful business development are slim without some knowledge of how the pieces function and of the process required to pull the pieces together. With the Internet, new tools are emerging almost daily. You'll need to know how to blend New Media and Web 2.0 tools with traditional business development to succeed in today's marketplace. Understanding what makes business development tick is essential whether you're doing it yourself or delegating it to someone else.

7. Lack of patience. "We ran an ad once and nothing happened." (Or substitute, "We went to that event once," or "We joined that group and nothing happened.") We've all heard that. But did you know that business development research shows that it takes between seven to 30 "touches" to make a sale? Customers won't buy until they have an urgent need. Until then, all you can do is create name recognition and a good reputation. That's the value of the Rule of 30. Business development

has a lot in common with farming. You wouldn't plant seeds one day and go out the next and dig them up in disgust because full grown plants hadn't sprouted overnight. Seeds take time to sprout. Business development seeds also take time to grow.

Putting the 30-Day Guide to Use

Business development success begins with RESULTS. The **RESULTS** approach stands for:

Recommit to business development.

Expect success.

Seek partners.

Understand your audience.

Look for win-win scenarios.

Take strategic action.

Stay visible.

In the next 30 days, you can see your productivity, networking, and business growth go from zero to zoom by applying the **RESULTS** formula.

Recommit to set aside at least 30 minutes each day (yes, weekends, too) to devote to developing your business development strategy for the next 30 days. (Thirty minutes is a minimum. Once you get started, you'll want to spend an hour, so block out the time now.)

Expect success by throwing yourself wholeheartedly into this 30-day commitment. If the little voice in the back of your head keeps saying, This is ridiculous. This isn't going to work, you are programming yourself for failure. Program yourself for success by writing down 30 things you would like to achieve from your online productivity and business development strategy. Some ideas include:

~ Reach new ideal prospects who may not know about your product/service and give them an incentive to learn more.

~ Gain visibility in local, regional, national, and professional media.

~ Position your company as the expert and leader in its field.

Considering these three examples, come up with your own list of 30 Success Expectations and keep them handy to check back on.

Seek partners. Success in the online world is just as dependent on partnership and collaboration as in the "real" world. These partners might be trusted vendors on whom you rely for your online business development tools, cloud computing applications, or mobile apps. They might also be companies in non-competing fields that serve the same customer base with whom you can create products and joint ventures.

Understand your audience in more profitable detail than ever before with the Action Items in Chapter 3. Make a list of 30 things you wished you knew about your best customers—and create 30 questions you can use for quizzes, surveys, and online discussions.

Look for win-win scenarios. As you're choosing programs to build your online business development platform and picking your productivity and networking tools, make sure to choose programs that are user-friendly, easy-to-use, and offer a good deal to both you and to your end users.

Take strategic action by putting what you learn in this book to work for you. As you read, be sure to do the Action Items at the end of each chapter. Complete all 30 chapter Action Items in the next 30 days and watch your online business development and productivity soar!

Stay visible by being consistently present in the live and virtual forums in which you network and seek new contacts. Create a list of 30 upcoming events, association meetings, or community programs where you could enhance your business visibility and seek to expand your contacts.

Most people put off doing business development because they think it's too difficult or too time-consuming. By using the principles in this book, you'll do more in 30 minutes a day for 30 days than most business owners do all year. That's the Get Results secret weapon—strategic, consistent effort in pursuit of clear, measurable results.

Results Reminder

!

Planning + Effort + Consistency = Results

Rule of 30

30

How many times are your messages "touching" prospects prior to making the sale? How close is that number to 30?

Action Items

1. Describe your primary target audience in detail: age, gender, education, location, income, key concerns, hobbies, aspirations, etc.

2. Justify why this is your primary audience. Now identify your secondary audience and explain why it's in second place. Look at your answers. Are they consistent with your ideal customer? With your current customers? How are they alike and different?

2
Your Profit Power Tool: The Business Plan

If the idea of creating a business plan makes your eyes glaze over, don't worry. This chapter isn't about the kind of detailed business plan you'd need to get a loan from a bank or money from a venture capitalist. In fact, the kind of business plan I'm going to show you just might be the most dynamic document you've ever created, and it is likely to be the most profitable.

First things first. If you've already written a business plan, print it out or dust it off and take a look at it. If it's more than two years old, its shelf life has expired. Why? Consumer expectations are constantly changing in response to economic conditions, new technology and lifestyle shifts. So be prepared to make some changes in your approach to ensure that it's up to date.

If you've never written a business plan, you're about to find out how to make it your most powerful business development tool. Pull out a pad of paper and a pen, and let's get started.

Define Success in Your Own Terms

Start off by defining what you mean by "success" for the next 12 months. Success can mean different things to different people. Your definition should be what will satisfy you, and it's likely to evolve over time. But unless you know what your success target is for the immediate future, you won't know when you've hit the mark.

Here are some ways to define business success for any given year:

~ Profit.

~ Market share.

~ New product penetration.

~ Media coverage and endorsements

~ National distribution channels.

~ Percent gain in product sales.

~ Industry credibility—speaking engagements, interviews, board or committee roles.

You may even think of a few more possibilities. The point is that success is more than just money, although for most companies and solo professionals, there is a target amount of money involved.

Ready, Aim...

Now write down your top three business goals for next year. Be sure to prioritize them from most important to least important. Do they match your definition of success?

One of the reasons business development often fails for small companies and solo professionals is that the business development and networking efforts are not aligned with the prioritized business plan goals. Overwhelmed business owners take whatever business development opportunities cross their paths, or join associations or professional groups without determining their potential benefit. They don't know how to say yes with confidence and no without guilt, because they don't have any standard to judge the opportunities.

Your business plan sets that standard. Next to each of your prioritized business goals, write down who the target audience is for that goal. The more precisely you can narrow down the target audience (instead of "everyone" it would be better to say "college educated men between the ages of 18 and 30"), the more precisely you'll be able to target your business development. You may have more than one target audience for each goal (for now), or you may have the same target audience for all of your goals. That's okay. We'll look at your audiences in more detail in the next chapter.

...Fire! Or Aim Again

Once you've matched an audience with a prioritized goal, make a list of all your current business development efforts. List everything: Websites, professional memberships, event sponsorships, trade shows, networking groups, banner ads, Facebook ads, online marketing efforts, direct mail, print or radio ads, signage, social media, e-mail newsletters, speaking appearances, online and traditional press release distribution, and so on. Now that you've made a comprehensive list, match each business development effort to the target audience it reaches, and to the business goal it supports. Do you see any disconnects?

Usually at this point, company owners notice that they have business development efforts that reach a particular target audience but aren't communicating a message that supports the business goal that is now linked to that audience. For example, perhaps paid magazine ads are reaching the right type of reader, but the call to action isn't aligned with the top business goal. If the goal is "increase the mailing list with opt-ins," the ad should encourage readers to go to the Website and sign up with their e-mail address to receive some kind of reward, such as a useful checklist, article, or mini e-book.

Sometimes, company owners discover "orphan" business development efforts that don't seem to connect with any prioritized business goal. "Orphan" business development efforts might exist out of habit, or because they met an old need, or because there's an emotional connection to the action or to the person who sold it to you. But if it's not advancing a business goal, it's an "orphan" because there is no reason to keep on doing it. They might also find business development efforts that are reaching the wrong audience.

Getting the effort in sync with the best target audience in support of the right prioritized goal is the first step to business development success. Online business development and networking efforts will be most successful if the message and effort are linked to the right goal and audience, and you'll get a multiplier effect on all of your business development efforts if they are all in sync. As you'll see when we get into the details, good online business development and networking not only help to raise your company's visibility, but also create lasting relationships and brand recognition that creates future orders. If those business development actions aren't tied to the right goals and audiences, your prospect will get a muddled, ineffective message that will cost you sales.

Look for Gaps

Now that you've aligned your business plan goals according to your success priorities, matched the goals to the right target audiences and matched your current business development efforts to the right audience/goal, it's time to go "gap hunting." Here's how to "gap hunt":

~ Are there any goals/audiences without any supporting business development efforts?

~ Are all the business development efforts bunched up around one goal?

~ Is most of your business development effort supporting your top prioritized goal?

~ Are you putting most of your effort into goals you've ranked as second or third in importance?

~ Do you have target audiences who aren't the focus of any business development?

~ Is one target audience getting all the business development messages?

~ Are second- or third-goal audiences getting more business development messages than your top goal audience?

Make a list of these business development gaps, because you'll need to address them in your strategy, and you'll want to look for ways online business development and networking can help you plug the holes.

Defining Your Transformative Value

Before any customer spends money, he or she has to overcome two obstacles: ego and money. Ego is what makes people try to fix a problem themselves, rather than hire someone. They don't agree to buy until they fail. Money is what clients hope to save by doing the job themselves. Most people won't hire someone for any job until 1) they have failed to do it themselves, and 2) there is enough at stake that continued failure will cost more than paying for the job.

Every person who buys your product does so because he or she has a problem. For example, if you are a business coach who specializes in work/life balance, your clients set aside time and money to work with you because their current balance isn't functioning well. If you run a roofing firm, clients hire you to replace missing shingles. Balance or missing shingles are the problem.

Behind the problem is a pain. That's the chance that the problem could get bigger. The work/life balance problem could begin to impact a person's relationships or ability to complete projects. A few missing shingles could lead to water damage and more expensive repairs if not fixed promptly.

Underneath the pain is a fear. The fear is the "what if" that keeps a prospect up at night envisioning the worst scenario. The work/life balance issue could lead to a divorce, delinquent children, and/or bankruptcy. Water damage could mean a whole new roof and expensive structural damage.

Your Transformative Value is the way you speak to the problem/pain/fear in your own unique way. When you make a sale, it's because you have done two things: successfully answered the ego/money challenge and satisfied the problem/pain/fear issue. To satisfy the ego/money challenge, you've convinced the prospect that you have skills they don't in order to save them money with better results. You've resolved the problem/pain/fear issue by assuring them that you can fix the initial problem so well that the pain and fear disappear. Speaking compellingly about your prospect's problem/pain/fear will make your networking and business development efforts more productive, yielding more results with less effort.

Successful business development efforts communicate your unique Transformative Value to your best prospects to satisfy both the ego/money objection and to solve the problem/pain/fear. Online business development and networking are two of the channels you can use to communicate that message effectively.

Results Reminder

! Invest most of your business development effort into achieving your number-one business goal.

Rule of 30

30

Can you identify 30 ways your business development speaks to your Transformative Value?

Action Items

1. Prioritize your top three business goals.
2. Match them to their target audience.
3. Match the business development to the goals/audience and gap hunt.
4. Determine the Transformative Value for each goal/audience.

3
Digging Into the Business Plan for Big Payoff

Let's spend a little more time talking about your target audiences before we move on, because the key to all business development is to give the right message to the right person. Matching the message to the target audience is still essential in online business development and networking, even though it may seem as if your information is reaching everyone on the Internet.

The first truth about business development is that it's easier and more cost efficient to go where your best target audience is already congregating, rather than trying to get them to form a new group. That's the thinking behind magazine, TV, and radio salespeople who show you a media kit that details who reads, watches, or listens to their product. The same thinking is true of trade shows, professional association memberships, and social media sites. You'll get more exposure for your money if you connect with a group that already exists rather than spending time and effort to build a brand-new group and attract people to it. And while connecting with new prospects is important, remember that you'll see real productivity gains by deepening relationships with existing clients to upsell them, win repeat business, or encourage referrals, rather than frantically trying to drum up new clients.

Unfortunately, most small businesses and solo professionals have been so busy handling whatever business comes in the door that they haven't stopped to really think about who their best customers really are. Even fewer have thought about who their customers *should* be in order to achieve their business goals.

Getting to Know All About You

In Chapter 1, you wrote down many details about your target audience(s). Take out that list, and compare it to the goal/audience/business development notes you made in Chapter 2. Here are some questions to ask:

~ Does your original audience profile match your new goal/audience/business development notes?

~ Are there second-level or third-level audiences you need to describe?

~ How well do the target audiences you have described match your current core customers? What are the similarities? What are the differences?

Now think about those prioritized business goals again. Your number-one business goal should reflect your definition for success this year. Is your current core customer likely to help you achieve your business goal?

Let me give you an example. Suppose you're a life coach, someone who helps people clarify their vision of success for their business or career. Right now, your calendar is full of people who coach with you for one or two one-hour sessions and then move on. Very few of them return as clients after their initial sessions. They like you and appreciate the results, but they say money is the reason they stop after just a few sessions.

Now suppose you have as your top business goal to take your clients further through a new five-week coaching program. You would like to charge more for the program than you do for the regular coaching sessions, and your goal factors in two desirable outcomes: 1) making more income from the same amount of time, and 2) locking in a longer income stream.

As happy as you've been with your current core customers, and as pleased as they've been with your work, it's not likely that they will be the best target audience for your new program. Why? It's probably out of their price range. That means you'll need to identify a new target audience for your business goal that is interested in what you have to offer and that can pay your increased price.

You also need to think about the clients you currently have who don't fit any of your business goal target audiences. Maybe they were among your first clients when you started your business, and your vision has changed as time moved on. Perhaps you took whoever walked in the door. Maybe some of them haven't been pleasant or profitable, or maybe the work you're doing for them no longer fits with your goals. You'll want to take a good look at their characteristics to avoid attracting more problem clients, and you certainly don't want to make them a target audience. It's your call as to whether you gently let the current misfit clients know that you can no longer serve their needs or whether you just let them gradually drift away, but it's just as helpful to be clear about who you *don't* want as it is to know specifically who you *do* want.

For any of your business development and networking activities to work at peak effectiveness, they need to focus not just on an audience that *could* buy your product, but on the audience that is the *absolute best match* for your product. There will always be some less-than-perfect clients who slip in around the edges, but you don't want to market to them. You want to market to your best customer.

People who were your best customers when you started out may not still be a good fit as your company grows and your goals change. That's okay. It's part of the life cycle of a business. You will save yourself time, energy, and money by knowing as much as you can about your best customer so that your message will be on-target to solve their problem/pain/fear. One of the scariest things for business owners is to shift their business development from an original target audience that met their needs when they were a start-up to a more precisely targeted audience that meets their goals today. But unless you change your audience to suit your goals, your networking is doomed to failure. Your outgrown audience just won't be able to meet your business needs, because your needs aren't in sync with their needs any more.

Make the shift by thinking about the qualities your new best target audience would have—their goals, their visions, and their problem/pain/fear. What will get them past the ego/budget wall? Now start to think about where those new audience members are already congregating. What kind of events are they going to? What clubs or associations do they belong to? What social media sites would attract them? What Websites do they visit frequently, where they might see a banner ad? How often do they search for the products and services you provide online, where they might see sponsored search results? Are they getting their information online or through traditional media? Do you know which media they are reading? (Once you know what online magazines and sites they read, you can target your PR to target those outlets.) Now is a good time to update your goals/target audiences with what you've just learned.

SWOT the Competition

When you first started your company, if you're like a lot of small companies, solo professionals, and home-based businesses, you focused on what you did best that people would pay for, and you may not have thought much about the competition. Now's a good time.

Think about the other companies you've encountered who provide products or services similar to yours. They could be local, regional, or national. The scope is determined by where your prospects are looking to find solutions more than it is by whether or not you consider yourself to be a regional or national company.

Here are some things to consider:

- ~ How many other companies provide a similar service locally?
- ~ How far will my prospects drive to obtain what I sell?
- ~ Can my prospects get what they need online or over the phone? (If so, you're competing regionally and nationally.)
- ~ What's different about my product/service/delivery than what my competitors offer? What's very similar?

~ How are the companies I admire providing the types
of products/services I'd like to provide a few years
from now?

~ How are other companies offering value and
convenience?

~ How do my materials or Website compare in profes-
sionalism to competitors?

~ What's special about the things I offer or the way I
do business to make my target prospect pick me over
someone else?

Now that you've put your thinking cap on, it's time to make
some notes. Take a piece of paper and divide it into four equal
boxes. Mark the boxes "Strengths," "Weaknesses," "Opportunities"
and "Threats." Now fill in the boxes from what you've just learned.

As you focus your networking message, you'll want to empha-
size your unique strengths (including your Transformational Value)
and go after opportunities (including your new best customers or
overlooked pockets of customers who need what you have to sell).
At the same time, you will need to be aware of your weaknesses and
watch out for threats.

Remember when I told you that everyone has a different definition for success? It's true about weaknesses and threats, too. One
"weakness" of your business may be that competitors sell at a lower
price. But if your price is justified by superior craftsmanship or materials, you could turn that weakness into a strength that becomes a
threat to your competitor's lower-quality product.

Threats, also, are a matter of perspective. If you are a personal
trainer, you might think that every other personal trainer in town
is a threat. However, the truth is that many of those trainers aren't
going after your target customer because they're chasing a different
target that fits their different goals. For example, if you specialize in
helping women stay active during and after pregnancy, and another
trainer specializes in training busy women executives, you might
turn that "threat" into a great two-way referral source as you refer
clients back and forth to each other as the clients go on maternity
leave and return to the workplace.

Results Reminder

! Know your competitors and your best customers as well as you know yourself.

Rule of 30

30

What are 30 characteristics of the prospects who best fit your number-one goal?

Action Items

1. Reassess your core customers in light of your prioritized business goals.

2. Update your target audiences to be the best prospects for achieving your new goals.

3. Now that you know your SWOT, look for hidden opportunities and strengths. For example, a high-integrity competitor might become a partner for collaboration, which turns a former threat into an ally. A current weakness might become a strength with a little adjustment. For example, a company that doesn't have a physical headquarters might think of that as a weakness, or they could reposition their ability to work with telecommuting staff and do virtual work for clients around the world as a strength.

4
Mining Networking Gems From the Business Plan

Now that you're clear on your goals, priorities, target audience, and SWOT, it's time to talk about money.

Budgeting Time and Money

Successful business development takes either cash or a cash equivalent. A cash equivalent is what you use instead of cash. It could be time that you barter, but more often than not, it's old-fashioned elbow grease. Business development requires time, and it also requires some money. If you have more time, you can save money. If you have less time, you can get the same work done by hiring help. One way or another, good business development is going to require investment.

I've heard business owners say that they had such a great location or product that they could "do business by accident." And I've driven past their location when it went up for sale after they went out of business. Success happens because of hard work, strategy and, yes, a little optimized luck. It doesn't happen by accident.

What do I mean by "optimized luck"? Optimized luck is what happens when you've done your homework, worked as hard as you can, and a great opportunity opens up in front of you. If you hadn't prepared yourself, you wouldn't be ready to make the most of the opportunity, or you might not even notice it. But you also didn't just get lucky. You prepared and trained so that you'd recognize luck when it showed up and so you would be ready to maximize your big break. It's definitely not "doing business by accident."

Take another look at your prioritized goals/target audiences/ current business development actions. If you've made a table, add another column for "cost." Write down what you think your current business development actions to reach that target audience and achieve that goal are costing you. The cost could be in time, or it could be in real money. It could be the cost of hiring someone to update your Website or design your brochure, or it could include printing, postage, advertising, or other fees. You could include membership dues for the groups you've joined to mingle with your target audience. Make the best estimates you can and then look at the results.

Here are a few questions to ask yourself:

~ How much are you currently spending for each goal?
~ Are you spending the most to achieve your top goal?
~ Where does your spending appear to be most productive in yielding results?
~ Is what you're spending worth the potential new revenue that goal could provide?
~ Could you spend more if it would achieve your goal faster?

You may see some opportunities to make a few course corrections. If you are spending more to achieve your third priority than you are for your top priority, you've got a problem. If you're spending more to achieve a goal with smaller revenue potential than for a goal with larger revenue potential, it's time to reconsider. If you're not spending anything, hoping to "do business by accident," you're on thin ice.

Online business development and networking becomes much more cost effective when it targets a highly defined audience. Your online networking efforts will also have more success when you know the habits of your audience well enough to provide information they want and need. By focusing, you'll stop wasting time and money on networking efforts that aren't reaching your ideal prospects or aren't offering what your prospects need to encourage them to make a purchase. Your highly targeted, strategic online networking efforts will be more successful because they give your prospects what they want and need. You gain by converting more prospects into customers while spending time and money more effectively.

How Much Is Enough?

I've seen all kinds of estimates on how a business development budget should be. Usually, the estimate is just enough to cover the products or services the person doing the estimate wants to sell.

An industry standard that's been around for a long time is 5 percent of revenue. The idea behind making your business development budget a percentage of your revenue is that business development, networking, and productivity enhancement costs are funds you are reinvesting into the company, and should be tied to how well the company is doing. In the real world, I've seen companies spend far less and far more than 5 percent and get results that met their definition of success. What matters most is that you spend your budget wisely.

A zero budget won't keep you in business long, and it certainly won't help you grow. If you truly have no cash, you'll need to roll up your sleeves and put sweat equity to work. If this describes your situation, how many hours can you put into doing business development? Write it down, and put a dollar estimate of your hourly rate next to it. That's what you're really spending.

If you're already spending money and you're comfortable with that level of investment, make sure that you've prioritized your budget in line with your prioritized goals. Put the biggest chunk of money where you'll get the best return or achieve the biggest goal. (This becomes a great way to say no without guilt to one of those "fabulous" business development opportunities a salesman presents to you.)

If you're willing to invest more to achieve your goals faster, or because you know that growth requires more resources, then determine a dollar amount you can spend and divide it among your prioritized goals. Budgeting money doesn't obligate you to spend it, but it does give you a tool to prioritize new opportunities, and it may free you to investigate options you might not have considered before you knew what was available to spend.

Remember that your efforts must be accounted for in your budget either in dollars or in time spent. As you budget your time to complete other projects, be sure to allow for your business development, productivity, and networking investment.

Setting a budget also creates one way to measure effectiveness. Over time, you'll want to ask yourself whether a particular productivity or networking method is earning its keep. Knowing what you've budgeted for it compared to the value of how it contributes to achieving your goal comes in handy when you need to decide what to keep and what to change.

The "Irresistible Difference"

Before we leave the nitty-gritty of your business plan, there's one item left we need to talk about, your "Irresistible Difference."

You already know your Transformational Value. That's how you address your prospect's problem/pain/fear and overcome his ego/money objection. Your Irresistible Difference is what draws a prospect to you and your company as opposed to your competitors. Your Irresistible Difference should tap directly into who your best prospect/customer is. It should fit that customer like their favorite pair of jeans, not only covering what's necessary, but making them feel wonderful as well.

Go back to your best customer's qualities. What can you provide in your service, package, or delivery that will meet their need as well as their unspoken desire? For some customers, convenience is king. For others, it's value, or reliability, or exceptional knowledge. Not only will you gain some good insights into powerful ways to make a networking connection by looking for the Irresistible Difference, but you'll also get some great ideas for where to find your best prospects and how to reach them.

For example, customers who prize value may join online communities dedicated to saving money. They could be great places for you to participate through chat, forum posts, and blogs because your audience is already there. A brand-conscious customer may place more than the usual value in being a member of professional and alumni associations and participating at a higher-than-average level. You might find those groups particularly useful to your business development strategy because they tap into qualities the prospect prizes.

Your Irresistible Difference demonstrates how well you understand the quality the prospect values through where you market (including your choice of online business development, social media, and PR), how you structure your product/service, how you deliver your product, and how you position your company in the marketplace.

As you become aware of the Irresistible Difference you offer to your different target audiences, make a note of it so you won't forget to put its power to work for you.

Results Reminder

! Effective business development isn't free. Prioritize your money and sweat equity and make it count.

Rule of 30

30

What are 30 different ways you could illustrate your Irresistible Difference to your prospects and customers?

Action Item

1. Determine your business development budget for each prioritized business goal. Make sure the biggest budget supports the top goal.

2. Figure out what you can really spend on business development this year in time and money. Split that among your prioritized goals.

3. Identify your Irresistible Difference and start thinking about where your best prospects are already congregating.

5
Creating a
Business Development
Action Plan

Now you're ready to create an action plan for your business development. Your action plan is the key to the rest of your 30-day success because it's your compass and checklist. Your action plan takes all the pieces you've put together so far and creates a way for you to make them happen. You won't achieve every item on your action plan in 30 days, but you can lay the groundwork to achieve them and make real progress toward your goal.

To be successful, your action plan needs to be detailed. Vague goals like "I want to bring in more business" are not helpful, because they lack sufficient detail to enable you to take action toward making the goal a reality.

Action plan items must also advance at least one business plan goal by addressing that goal's target audience. You've already attached business development actions to each goal/ audience. This is a good time to look at those business development actions and break them into smaller steps. That will give you a better idea of the time and money—and specific actions— necessary to make them happen.

For example, perhaps your top business plan goal is to get more visibility about your products and services. You've identified the target audience, and you've decided to use the Internet to reach them. That's a step in the right direction, but not enough to really get you going.

Let's break "use online business development and networking" into several action steps.

~ Identify the Websites, blogs, and online membership sites where your ideal prospect is already a regular. These may present more productive opportunities for online networking and for getting your news and announcements in front of a more attuned audience.

~ Understand what circumstances or events trigger your customer to make a purchase. For example, if your customer values product reviews, it makes sense to put effort into getting your product reviewed by a reputable Website or by boosting your own networking visibility by writing guest blog posts or articles on review sites.

~ Determine what kinds of social media and online networking activities your customer is already involved in. How "wired" is your customer? How often do they use the Internet and devices such as smartphones or iPads in their daily routine?

~ Build on the e-mail list of your current customers, with whom you already have permission to communicate. What can you offer new prospects to encourage them to opt in to your newsletter list? Getting opt-in permission supports your ongoing networking, since it gives you permission to stay in touch.

~ Take a look at your ability to remain productive, even when you're on the road or away from the office. What could work better? Where are there frequently breakdowns in productivity?

~ Think about how you are currently seeking to meet new ideal prospects (networking). Are you taking full advantage of social media and online networking opportunities to reach a broader audience?

Do you see how action steps take your business development from being a great idea to something tangible? As you read through the rest of the chapters in the book, don't just write down business development ideas—turn those ideas into step-by-step action plans and attach them to the appropriate prioritized business goal and its target audience. This one step will make an amazing difference in the results you see from your online business development and networking because it will make it clear what you can do every day to make your goals happen.

Results Reminder

! If a goal or a business development strategy seems too daunting, break it down into action steps and then tackle one step at a time in sequential order to make it happen!

Rule of 30

30

Your daily 30 minutes for business development, productivity, and networking should always advance or achieve one of your top priority action plan items.

Action Item

Take a fresh look at the business development actions you identified. Can you break each business development action into at least three to five action plan steps that could be handled in 30 minutes a day?

6
Finding Your Real Story and True Voice

Have you ever noticed how some companies seem to change who they are and how they sound with each new marketing campaign or elevator speech? Even worse, have you ever seen a company portray a totally different personality depending on whether you go to its Website, read a brochure, see its at a trade show, or meet its employees in person at a networking event?

Many companies have a mish-mash of marketing materials and networking identities that have been created over time, often by many different people. Some companies seem to lurch from strategy to strategy, never investing the time to allow any single approach to take root and pay off. Customers become confused, because the company doesn't seem to know its own identity. Even worse, a company that seems to change its personality every month can seem insincere, even untrustworthy.

The Internet complicates this disconnect, because it's easier than ever for prospects to hop from site to site, and if your company's personality seems to change between your Website, blog, online brochure, articles, and social media sites, your prospect will start to wonder who the real you is. Customers know when the tone of your in-person or online networking doesn't match the rest of their experience with your firm, or when the story they heard at a trade show isn't consistent with what they see on your Website.

One of the easiest ways to fix this is to discover the Real Story of your company, and the True Voice that is uniquely yours.

Telling Your Real Story

Remember the problem/pain/fear that drives your prospect past ego and money objections to seek out help? Your Real Story should demonstrate how you have solved a very similar problem/pain/fear for someone else, someone the reader can relate to.

The story format is especially powerful for sharing this information because human beings, even in the Internet age, are hard-wired to listen to stories. Stories sell.

Networking and marketing efforts incorporate your Real Story as a way to make an emotional connection with readers and differentiate your firm from others in the same industry. The essence of your Real Story should also permeate your online business development efforts with a personality that is unique to your company.

What is the story of your business? If you don't think your business has a story to tell, here are five ways to uncover your Real Story:

~ The owner's story. Some types of stories reach very deep into the American consciousness. Stories about second chances, self-made successes, hard-working newcomers who realize the American dream, and reinvention speak to very deeply held beliefs about who we are. I knew a business owner who came to the United States as an exchange student from China, and received her education and met her husband here. Because of the gift of a pearl necklace from an aunt back in China who knew a pearl farmer, this woman and her husband now own a pearl importing and jewelry design business. Her story of reinvention and adaptation while retaining her roots has gotten her media coverage and positive exposure for her business.

~ The product's story. What need does your product meet? The owner of a chain of coin-operated laundries I knew realized that he doesn't just give people clean clothes—he helps them show their love for their families and succeed in the workplace by having a neat and clean appearance. In his city neighborhood of recent immigrants who are climbing the ladder of prosperity, family and self-respect are very deeply held values. Do your services or products offer people security, good health, or a chance to succeed? What is the need that prompts your customer to buy?

~ The business's story. Has your business overcome adversity? We cheer for the businesses that found a way to come back after 9/11 in the TriBeCa neighborhood of New York City or after Hurricane Katrina in New Orleans. Has your company weathered bad times, lopsided competition, succession crises, or problems and come back stronger than ever? People love a comeback story. (Notice that Rocky Balboa has six movies!)

~ Your customers' stories. Go beyond testimonials. A case study tells the story of the problem and how your company solved it—but it's really a story about a hero, a dragon, and a damsel in distress. The dragon is the business problem—for example, a project badly behind schedule and over budget. Your company is the hero. The client is the damsel in distress. Every good adventure has a few plot twists to keep our interest—what challenges happened on the way to slaying the dragon? Did you lose key project personnel when you needed them most? Did a piece of crucial equipment break or get delayed in shipping? Details like this make your story compelling. And then there's the happy ending—how your company solved the problem and what it meant for the customer—in the form of significant dollar savings, productivity enhancement, the ability to compete in new markets. Help listeners feel the real benefit.

~ The story of your mission. Is your company part of your mission in life? Do you want to make the world a better place through the product or service you provide? Perhaps you became a lawyer because someone in your family was taken advantage of, and you want to make sure that others receive justice. Maybe you learned martial arts because you were robbed and ended up opening a studio to teach others to be safe. Your mission goes beyond your personal story to have a broader impact and make a difference in the world around you. Even the most mundane business can have a mission. Maybe you repair cars, but your commitment is to keep people from being endangered by breakdowns or from losing their jobs because of unreliable transportation. How do you make a difference?

Telling the Real Story of your business makes a powerful connection with potential customers, which is pure gold when it comes to networking and relationship-building. It can differentiate you from competitors in ways they can't copy. Once you uncover your Real Story, it affects the way you communicate about your business and the way you think about yourself, your products, and your customers.

The Power of Your True Voice

Many people put off business development activities for their companies because they don't feel authentic when they are in sales mode, or they believe that networking is inherently untruthful and pushy. How would you feel about networking if it felt completely authentic and truthful? Would you be able to overcome any childhood instructions not to "blow your own horn" or boast if the words seemed natural, honest, and comfortable?

Using your True Voice to communicate your message as you network feels natural, sounds authentic, and just seems to flow. The True Voice of your business is in the words that seem to show up again and again in the way you describe your company, the way others introduce you and your company, and the way clients express their appreciation for what your company does for them. Many companies never recognize or harness their True Voice, so their marketing materials and networking spiel sound contrived, generic, or insincere.

Here are five tips to find and use the True Voice of your business:

~ Listen to yourself. The next time you make your networking introduction, listen to yourself as you talk. If you have developed an elevator speech, write it down and take a good look. What verbs are you using? What adjectives? What nouns? Make a list—you'll come back to it as you work through the tips.

~ Listen to your clients. Take some of your best clients to lunch and ask them to tell you what they like about your company. Explain that you are rethinking your business development efforts and want to make sure you are on target. Or, pull out the comment cards and e-mails sent by happy customers and look at the words they use. Once again, jot down the nouns, verbs, adjectives, and phrases that show up. Do some appear more than once? Underline the words and phrases that are used frequently.

~ Listen to your employees. Ask your best employees what they like most about what they do. Ask them to tell you about how they help customers. Ask them to describe the business, your products, the solutions you provide. What problem or need do they think they are solving? Add the key words and phrases to your list.

~ Listen to your friends. If you are introduced at a business function by one of your colleagues, what words do they use to describe your business and your service? What problem do they say you solve? Read over your own marketing materials. Do the same solutions or phrases pop up frequently? Write them down.

You now have a list of key words and phrases that naturally describe what you do, who you serve, and what benefit you provide. To use your True Voice, take the most powerful words from your list and look for ways to use those words and phrases throughout your spoken and written communications for greater effectiveness (which improves your networking productivity).

When you use these True Voice words and phrases, you will feel honest and comfortable, because the words spring from who you really are and from the mission of your company. You'll find that the words make it easy to differentiate your services, because they come from your strengths and from the tangible benefits you have provided to your customers.

Using the True Voice of your business will make your message unique, compelling, and natural, in both your online business development and in your online and offline PR. You'll also feel more comfortable and confident sharing your information in a voice that feels right to you.

Results Reminder

Your Real Story told in your True Voice is memorable, credible, and compelling.

Rule of 30

30

What are 30 different words or phrases that come naturally as you talk about your product, service, and results?

Action Items

1. Identify your strongest Real Story. Brainstorm ways you can share it through the power of PR. Text is good, but audio and video are also very powerful and can be included as links in press releases and article pitches

2. Be sure to look at your most successful banner ads, brochures, Webpages, and sales materials as you compile your list of 30 True Voice words and phrases.

3. Once you've compiled your list, keep it handy as you develop your networking messages and online membership profile content so you remember to use your True Voice words and phrases.

7
Touches to Transactions

Modern business development wisdom holds that in to-day's advertising-saturated world, it takes at least seven to 30 "touches," or reminders, before a consumer takes action. Although that may seem like a lot when you first hear it, if you think about how you act when you're the consumer, it begins to make sense.

Your online networking can account for several of those 30 touches (social media, online marketing, and Internet PR can provide even more touches). But to be effective, you need to think about how touches become transactions.

Touches and Trigger Points

We manage to ignore tens of thousands of advertising messages every day, mostly because they promote products we aren't currently interested in buying. The key term here is "currently." When you realize you need a product or service, suddenly you tune into the messages related to the product/ service that you had been screening out.

The situation that changes everything is a trigger point. It's an event that moves you from being someone who hasn't thought about making a purchase or who has been casually window shopping to someone who needs to buy right now. The seller usually can't change the trigger point (although they try to influence it with education, sales, and specials), but you can make sure you're making enough touches so that when a triggering event moves a prospect from looker to buyer, he or she will think about your company.

Let's use a car purchase as an example. If your car is reasonably new and in good working order, you may not be thinking about buying a new car. You probably tune out car ads, e-mails from dealerships, or radio commercials about great specials. Or maybe you've been thinking about buying a new car—sometime. You might be casually reading car ads, visiting dealer Websites, paying some attention to commercials, even slowing down when you pass the dealer's lot for a good look. You may even meet someone from the dealership at a networking event and make a positive connection. But for now, it's all still window shopping.

Then a triggering event occurs. Your existing car is in an accident, and it will cost more to fix it than it's worth. Suddenly, you're in the market for a new car, and you need it right now.

Until that triggering event happened, there wasn't much the car dealers could do to hurry up your purchase. You bought the car based on your schedule of when you needed one, not on the dealership's schedule of when it wanted to sell one. Business owners often forget that it's the customer's need that drives the purchase cycle more than it is driven by sales and specials. But there's a very important thing to remember: When a customer moves from shopper to buyer, the company that has made the most touches through networking and marketing is first in line to get his or her business.

Go back to the car example. When that prospect was window shopping, the dealership with the best Website, or the showroom that was polite about a test drive without a commitment (a form of networking) is likely to be the first place that prospect goes when he or she moves from shopper to buyer. Those touches pay off in top-of-mind awareness.

Where does online networking come in? Well-placed online networking is a low-pressure way to remain in the forefront of a prospect's awareness with touches where there's interest but no trigger for an immediate purchase. It can also keep your company in touch with current customers so that when add-ons or upgrades become necessary, you're first in line for the business. Regular, strategic online networking increases your company's visibility and extends your credibility as an expert. Both visibility and credibility are important to future sales, since prospects must remember you and must believe that you provide a quality product or service.

The key here is not to view online networking as a way to provide a barrage of "buy now" messages. Instead, think of how you can engage the prospect in a conversation about whatever product or service you sell, with the immediate focus on offering helpful information related to the problem/pain/fear.

Some examples of this might include being consistently present through networking, making helpful comments on blogs related to your industry, and contributing bylined content on Websites that your ideal prospect uses frequently. If your customer is constantly on the go, a well-timed mobile text ad might encourage a convenience purchase or entertainment choice. A great e-newsletter can extend the conversation with a prospect or customer, gather valuable feedback, and provide subtle education about the benefits of the products and services you offer. With an autoresponder, you can send a targeted series of follow-up e-mails to draw a new prospect further down your sales funnel. A good online shopping cart can suggest related products that a purchaser might wish to add to the order, or provide a "thank-you" coupon or discount to encourage a future purchase. Making a personal connection on professional networking sites can help put a face to the name. The more you hone your networking productivity, the more time you'll be able to devote to effective business development.

While you usually can't close a sale before the customer has experienced a trigger point, once you've established a relationship, you have the chance to educate the prospect about that trigger point. Perhaps the best time to buy a new piece of equipment isn't when the old equipment falls apart. Perhaps there are trade-in advantages or depreciation advantages to buying on a shorter purchase cycle. Maybe you can point out benefits that deal so much better with the problem/pain/fear than the old product that the prospect decides to buy sooner rather than later. You've altered the trigger point through education, and because your company provided the information in an ongoing relationship, you're likely to be first in line to get the sale.

When someone connects to you on a networking site, subscribes to your e-newsletter, blog, Facebook page update, or Twitter feed, they're agreeing to get updates (information) from you on a regular basis. If you share information that speaks to his or her needs, every update does double duty; it reminds the prospect about you (a touch) while it provides useful information (deepening your relationship and educating to alter the trigger point). Online networking makes it easier and less expensive (and less intrusive) than ever before to stay in contact as touches prepare for a trigger.

Results Reminder

!

Using a touch strategy keeps you visible by providing useful information your targeted audience wants and needs without sales pressure.

Rule of 30

30

What content can you offer to provide 30 valuable touches?

Action Items

1. Your online networking touches can introduce prospects to your Website, shopping cart, e-newsletter, blog, or other sites. How could you use these touches to deepen your relationship with prospects?

2. Is there something you can offer prospects who have their triggering event that would provide value for their decision-making process?

3. What content can you communicate through online networking that would increase your credibility and build trust prior to the prospect's triggering event? Is there information you can share to alter the trigger point through education?

8
Productivity Basics: Cloud Computing

The term "cloud computing" sounds intangible, and that's just the point. "Cloud computing" refers to access to software that is accessible via subscription over the Internet. Programs that reside in the cloud are actually housed on the servers of the company that owns the software and which provides subscription access. Unlike traditional software, such as word processing or spreadsheet programs that are stored on your computer's hard drive, programs that reside in the cloud never have to be installed, updated, or uninstalled from your computer. That's the beauty of the cloud.

Why Move to the Cloud?

Why would you want your software to be housed on the cloud? Several good reasons come to mind:

~ You don't have to install the program, so you can use software that requires greater speed or memory than your desktop or laptop might possess.

~ Because the software is stored on the cloud, it doesn't hog memory or bog down your computer.

~ You don't have to worry about updating the software; the tech staff at the company providing the software takes care of that.

~ Because you access the software via the Internet (and a secure password), you can access your software (and possibly your related files) from any computer, anywhere you have an Internet connection.

~ Because your access is via subscription (usually monthly or annually), your costs are much less than if you were to purchase a private license for the program.

~ When you no longer want or need the software, you simply cancel the subscription. There is no software to uninstall from your computer.

~ If there's a problem with the software, your subscription includes access to technical support. It's the provider's responsibility to fix the bugs, and you don't have to download patches or new versions.

Starting to see the appeal? Cloud computing programs offer extremely flexible access to powerful programs without the hassles of maintaining the software on your own computer. If you've ever suffered through a lengthy software download (especially one that needed to be redone several times), you'll understand the appeal of being able to "visit" your software instead of needing to have it all on your hard drive.

What kinds of programs reside in the cloud? During the last decade, a growing variety of programs have become available via cloud computing. Most, if not all, of the productivity and networking programs I'll talk about in the remainder of the book are cloud computing programs. Here are just some of the types of programs provided via cloud computing:

~ Calendar programs, such as Google Calendar and Tungle.

~ E-mail programs, such as Constant Contact.

~ Web audio/video programs, such as AudioAcrobat.

~ Conferencing programs, such as GoToWebinar.

~ Shopping cart programs, such as 1ShoppingCart.

~ Data storage programs, such as Carbonite.

~ Online job management programs, such as Elance.

~ Benefits administration programs, such as BaseOnline.com.

What About Security on the Cloud?

If the idea of having your valuable and proprietary data residing in the cloud worries you, there are steps you can take to set your mind at ease. First, make sure that you understand the individual service provider's privacy policies, terms of use, intellectual property safeguards, and recommended methods for assuring the security and integrity of your data.

Second, always back up essential information. This can mean creating a printout, saving a Web-based document as a file or a screen shot, or copying essential information to your hard drive or an FTP (file transfer protocol) storage site. An FTP site allows you to store and share documents or files that are too large for regular e-mail. Yes, FTP sites are also cloud computing sites. (An example is 4shared.com, but there are many similar sites.)

Third, be certain to safeguard your password. Realize that when you share access to your cloud computing sites with an administrative assistant or colleague, they may gain access to your billing and credit card information unless the site allows for different levels of access. Some cloud computing sites offer a group membership, so that you can provide access to several employees or partners while keeping your own account information private. Other programs make it possible to designate an administrator who can access everything except the billing/payment information. If you must share your password with an assistant, keep track of which passwords have been shared and be sure to change your password if your relationship with the assistant ends.

Cloud computing programs can boost your productivity by giving you access to powerful software without the hassle of downloads and updates. You save time, reduce the in-house need for online storage, and reduce your dependence on hired computer professionals. Just think—no more losing part of a day as your IT consultant tinkers with the settings to make sure a newly downloaded program doesn't wreck your network!

Small businesses and solo professionals also benefit by gaining access to valuable online services and software which would be prohibitively expensive to license on an individual basis, and which would require significant investment in servers and personnel to install and manage in-house.

For big productivity gains and lower costs, get into the cloud!

Results Reminder

!   Gain several hours a year when you "outsource" software installation and updates to cloud computing providers!

Rule of 30

30

What are the 30 computerized tasks you perform most often?

Action Item

Can you find cloud computing programs to perform all or any of your 30 most frequent computerized tasks? How do they compare in cost to what you have now? If you were able to save just an hour a year per program, you gain almost a week's productivity!

9
Virtual Calendar and Scheduling

Virtual calendar programs enable you to track your appointments and other commitments via computer, rather than in a manual date book. Scheduling programs make it possible for you to share access to your calendar with others to take the back-and-forth out of finding good times and dates for meetings and phone calls. Whether you prefer to access your calendar from your computer, smartphone, or tablet PC, virtual calendar and scheduling programs mean you never have to say, "I left my datebook back at the office."

Virtual Calendar and Scheduling Basics

Virtual calendar programs look and act just like their paper counterparts, with two important exceptions: they are accessible via computer, and most allow some level of sharing so that you can invite participants to meetings and note the appointment simultaneously on your calendar and theirs.

At a minimum, your virtual calendar should make it easy for you to enter new appointments, change or cancel existing appointments, and block out time when you are unavailable. Many programs also alert you to upcoming appointments via e-mail reminders or pop-ups on your screen, making it less likely that you'll miss a meeting.

As users take computing on the go, virtual calendar programs have evolved to include smartphones and tablet PCs as well as laptops and desktops. Some programs can populate all your linked devices with your schedule, while other programs can be accessed online from any device with Internet capability. No matter what device you use to access them, virtual calendar programs enable you to keep your calendar close at hand and update your schedule wherever you are.

Calendar sharing and scheduling programs save you time and increase your productivity by taking out the middleman when it comes to making appointments. Tired of trading e-mails with clients or vendors to set up meeting times or phone calls? Using a calendar sharing/scheduling program makes it easy to share a calendar with your available days and times with others and to have them select the best options from your openings and book the appointment. Some calendar programs enable you to share different versions of your schedule with different groups of people, so you could, for example, separate work and personal appointment times.

If you've ever spent hours playing phone or e-mail "tag" trying to confirm an appointment, the productivity benefits of a sharable, online calendar become immediately apparent. If you make just five appointments per week and each appointment now takes you an average of 15 minutes to arrange, using an online calendar and scheduling program could save you five hours a month!

Taking a Tour of Some Top Programs

There are plenty of online calendars and scheduling programs to choose from, with more being added every day. Here, we'll take a quick tour of four popular programs to get a feel for what's available.

You may not realize it, but if you use Microsoft Outlook, you've already got an online calendar that's linked to your e-mail and Outlook's integral Business Contact Manager. Access the calendar at the bottom of your Outlook dashboard. You'll find well-marked buttons that enable you to add an appointment or create a meeting with multiple invitees. You can invite someone to your meeting by accessing contacts in your e-mail address book or the program's Business Contact Manager, or by entering the person's e-mail address manually.

You'll be able to differentiate between all-day events and regular appointments, and to set recurring appointments. If the other people you want to invite to a meeting have shared their calendars with you, you can view their calendars to look for available times and dates before scheduling the meeting, to avoid conflicts and rescheduling.

Because Outlook's calendar is linked to your e-mail, you'll get pop-up meeting reminders when you log into Outlook. You can access your calendar when you don't have an Internet connection, although you won't be able to invite others. Outlook allows you to adjust the time increments and designate work days and non-work days, for those whose meetings don't automatically fall on the hour or half-hour, and for people whose weekends don't fall on Saturday and Sunday.

There's even an easy way to auto-populate your Outlook calendar with the major U.S. holidays at the touch of a button. And if you've entered personal details, such as birthdays and anniversaries, in your Business Contact Manager, your Outlook calendar can pull in that data so you never forget a special day!

Google offers a free online calendar with plenty of robust features. With Google Calendar, you can create and share your schedule and view other people's Google Calendars. Google offers a built-in synchronization feature that enables you to see and access your calendar from your mobile phone as well as your computer, and share updates made on one device with the calendar stored on the other device.

As with Outlook, Google Calendar makes it easy to invite others to meetings and confirm their attendance. It's accessible for read-only viewing offline, so you can see where you need to go even if you're in a Wi-Fi dead zone. Google Calendar will send you reminders by e-mail and text message, and it can even sync with some other calendar programs, such as Outlook.

Apple's iCloud replaces its previous MobileMe virtual calendar. iCloud works with all Apple devices and shares books, photos, music, and apps as well as calendar information, e-mail and contacts. The iCloud is a hybrid virtual storage and virtual Swiss Army Knife of sorts, bringing together all of a user's data to make it location and device independent.

Because all data is stored on the iCloud, Apple takes care of syncing your devices for you. That's handy if you make an appointment using your iPad and want to later see your schedule using your computer or your iPhone. You can share your calendar with other iCloud users, and any changes will be automatically pushed out to the schedules of all meeting or event participants. The iCloud is an attempt to seamlessly integrate your online life, so the program also makes it possible for you to access your e-mail and phone contacts, virtual notes, online reminders, and Web bookmarks from all your devices.

Tungle is a stand-alone program (free, as of this writing) to share your calendar with people who may not be on the same e-mail program, such as people outside your organization. Tungle is especially designed for setting up meetings without hassle, and promises to help users avoid double-bookings and missed appointments.

The Tungle calendar makes it easy to limit your availability to particular days and times. This is handy if you want to reserve portions of your calendar for other work or events, or just want to control how much of your calendar can be booked by others. Tungle adjusts for differences in time zones and sends you reminders of upcoming appointments. Tungle also offers a difference between the private and public view of your calendar, meaning that your clients won't be privy to any personal appointments you book on your online calendar.

Tungle will sync with a variety of other calendar programs, including Outlook, Google Calendar, BlackBerry, LotusNotes, Facebook, and Apple iCal, among others. There's also a handy Tungle app for your smartphone so you can Tungle on the go.

Other programs similar to Tungle include TimeBridge and Doodle (calendar sharing), and Evite (event/party invitations).

Results Reminder

! Scheduling appointments via phone and e-mail can lead to confusion and frustration. Use virtual calendars and scheduling to simplify your life and end "appointment tag."

Rule of 30

30

List the 30 people with whom you most frequently set appointments. Be sure to include colleagues, clients, and vendors, as well as your family, medical providers, and recurring school, sports, or personal care appointments.

Action Items

1. Add your 30 most frequent appointment contacts to your virtual calendar list for easy scheduling.

2. Set up your virtual calendar for at least three months at a time. Make sure to include holidays, conferences, vacations, and other out-of-office events.

3. Sign up for a virtual scheduling program to eliminate phone and e-mail tag and reduce missed appointments.

10
Remote Computer Access and Storage

When you're on the go, it's difficult to bring all your files with you. Carrying a laptop can be difficult when traveling through airports, and taking your computer with you puts you at risk for theft and damage. Printouts are cumbersome, offer data security risks, and provide only a static snapshot.

To address these problems, cloud computing programs make it possible for users to access their computers remotely and store files in secure storage sites that can be accessed on the go. For users who rely on instant, mobile access to stored data but don't want to lug their laptops everywhere they go, these programs offer portability, security, and easy access.

Virtual Access to Your Computer, From Anywhere

GoToMyPC enables subscribers to securely access their computer back at the office while they're on the road. If you've ever had a moment of panic as you realized that you left the folder or the flash drive you needed for your out-of-office presentation back on your desk, you can appreciate the appeal. GoToMyPC is compatible with both Microsoft and Apple computers, and can also be accessed from an iPad. The service offers access to files, e-mail, applications, and network resources via a secure, encrypted connection. Other virtual access programs include LogMeIn, PCAnywhere and Anyplace-Control.

You'll need to weigh the convenience of remote access against the possibility, however slim, that even the most secure data connections can (at least theoretically) be compromised. If you travel frequently and have ever had a deal compromised by a missing file, the benefits may be well worth the risk to you. This is especially true for one-person companies who lack the office staff to e-mail or overnight a forgotten document.

If you're in a business in which a security breech would be catastrophic, it's probably worth the price to confer with your IT (information technology) consultant to explore options. While the remote access programs themselves may be secure, there are inherent security risks in using public access computers, such as those in hotels, libraries, and office supply stores. Only you can decide whether the risks outweigh the convenience. If you're not sure how to assess the risks, talk to your IT consultant.

Off-Site Storage on the Cloud

Corporations store their data backup in salt mines and high-security off-site locations. That's a little extreme (and expensive) for most small businesses, but the need for secure storage and backup isn't limited to large corporations. A flood, fire, or natural disaster could wipe out your computer and your locally stored flash drives and portable hard drives. Frequent backups to a storage location reduce your risk of a catastrophic data loss.

Storage capacity is another challenge for many users. While storage costs have decreased tremendously, making terabytes of capacity reasonably priced, some users rapidly exceed their on-site storage capability. Fortunately, cloud computing offers alternatives for both data security and data storage.

Carbonite, Mozy, MyOtherDrive, iBackup, Dropbox, Google Docs, GoDaddy, Sugarsync, ElephantDrive, LiveDrive, MyPCBackup, and other sites offer cloud-based data backup and storage capabilities. Most sites provide automated backup, making it less likely that you'll forget to update files. In addition, files stored on the cloud can be accessed from any location, giving you portability.

When looking into cloud-based data storage, remember that you're entrusting your sensitive files to a third party. Here are some questions to consider as you weigh your alternatives.

- ~ What happens to my data if the provider is sold, acquired, or goes out of business?
- ~ How does the provider assure site security?
- ~ What precautions are taken against hackers?
- ~ How does the provider do its own backup to assure my data is safe if the provider has a catastrophic event at their location?
- ~ What do other users say about ease of use, security, and customer support?

Cloud-based storage and backup can be valuable and affordable services. Having your files saved from just one on-site disaster could well be worth the investment in monthly fees. As always, be sure to check out provider options to find the service that is the best fit for your business.

Results Reminder

!

Make sure you are routinely backing up your data and storing it in a disaster-proof location.

Rule of 30

30

What 30 documents would be crucial for your business to have in order for it to continue in the event of a disaster?

Action Items

1. Think about the situations in which remote access might benefit your company. Check out providers and costs, then assess whether or not it's right for you.

2. Take a look at your current data backup and storage solutions. Can they grow with you as your company grows? Do they make it easy to access stored files and do frequent, regular data backups?

11
Skype and Other Virtual Phone Options

Question: When is a computer not a computer? Answer: When it's acting like a phone.

Thanks to voice over internet protocol (VOIP), it is possible to transmit voice data over high-speed Internet connections, utilizing the built-in microphone and speaker of devices ranging from laptop computers to cell phones to TV sets. VOIP is often less expensive than traditional landline or cell phone plans, especially for international calling. Even better, many providers offer free calling among members of their service.

Skype, Vonage, and Google Talk are just three of many VOIP providers in a rapidly growing field. While cell phone plans have dropped in price and have drastically reduced or eliminated domestic long-distance charges, international calling remains difficult. Cell phones either don't work for international calls or incur very high roaming charges. If your business involves frequent international calling, consider VOIP as an addition to or replacement for your current phone carrier.

VOIP requires that you have fairly current computer hardware as well as a broadband Internet data connection. Make sure you check the provider's specifications to assure that your connection speed and hardware will work with their service. Levels of VOIP service have also multiplied as VOIP has gained in popularity. Some are free, while other plans range from per-minute charges to flat monthly rates, so be sure you've assessed the cost of your current usage. You might also want to survey the clients you call most often to see which providers they are already using, and pick the service favored by the majority of your international customers.

Virtual phone programs have added an increasing number of extra services beyond cheap phone calls. Video conferencing and call recording have become widely available at very low rates, and offer additional ways to remain in touch and add a personal element to your long-distance client relationships.

As VOIP has matured, providers have added the ability to make calls via cell phones and even landlines. Pricing and conditions vary, so check to make sure the provider you are considering will work with your cell phone package or existing telephone service. Some providers bundle voice calling with other features such as live chat and group video conferencing.

When you are considering virtual phone options, don't base your decision solely on your current needs. If you haven't had access to video conferencing, think about how you might use it for client meetings, small group presentations, Webinars, or even connecting with employees working in remote locations. This might be a perfect time to add affordable communication options that make it easy for you to deepen your long-distance business relationships.

If you do choose a virtual phone provider, make sure you list your new phone number so that it is easy for others to reach you. If you prefer to use VOIP only for specific situations (such as international calling), you may want to share your phone number more selectively, or note a preference for what types of calls use your VOIP number, and which should call in on your traditional phone line.

Virtual phone services bring to life the "videophone" concept that was once just science fiction and make it both real and affordable. Whether you use VOIP for inexpensive video conferencing, recorded calls, or low-cost international calling, it's definitely worth a second look.

Results Reminder

! Free international calling can make it easy and affordable for you to grow your client base without geographic boundaries!

Rule of 30

30

Who are the 30 people you call long-distance most often? How do VOIP options compare with your current phone plan?

Action Item

Take a look at the virtual phone services that are available, and compare their costs and range of services with what you're currently using. Would you save money by adding VOIP services? Would you gain new and valuable communication capabilities?

12
Virtual Meeting Spaces and Teleconferencing

In today's world, it's what you know, not where you're located, that counts. Many companies work with a network of virtual contributors who are spread out across town, across the country, or across the world. Other companies have clients and prospects who are scattered all over the world, and struggle to find effective, low-cost ways to make a personal connection.

Webinars, Teleseminars, and Virtual Meetings

Not too long ago, the idea of video-conferencing was something only very large corporations could afford. Back in the day, video- or audio-conferencing required dedicated facilities, a trained audio-visual staff, and a serious investment in technology and equipment. Today, anyone with a phone and a computer that has a Webcam can run a virtual conference, and costs run from free to less than $100 for a system that will allow approximately 100 attendees, to a few thousand dollars for a top-of-the-line system able to host a much larger audience.

Webinars make it possible to gather a group together in a password-protected online area and share both voice and a slide or video presentation in real time. Many Webinar programs allow users to share control of the pointer or broadcast a live view of a single user's computer screen for the rest of the group to see. Some programs also have an online whiteboard where participants can write notes or draw diagrams. Webinars require a computer and a fast Internet connection from both host and attendees. Although many programs make it very easy to set up and attend a Webinar, it does require a basic level of computer literacy to host or attend a Webinar comfortably.

Teleseminars are audio-only meetings, training classes, or seminars held over phone lines without a visual component. They are simple to run and require no technical expertise beyond the ability to dial a phone. Teleseminars do not need a computer to run, as long as the host and participants can call into a prearranged conference line. If your audience is iffy on computer skills, a teleseminar may be the best way to go.

Virtual meetings usually involve a small work group rather than an invited crowd of hundreds. Most virtual meetings bring together a team of coworkers who are geographically distributed. Virtual meetings usually place a premium on being able to share documents and whiteboard space, and to collaborate in real time.

Plenty of Options

Today's Webinar, teleseminar, and virtual meeting software is available in a wide variety of options and pricing. Because this book is focused on the needs of small businesses and solo professionals, I'll forego discussion of some of the larger programs that offer corporate-level bells and whistles for a corporate-level price, and focus on the less expensive, subscription-based cloud computing programs that offer robust choices for a low monthly fee.

GoToWebinar, Yugma, and Instant Teleseminar are all popular, cloud-based programs that enable anyone to set up a Webinar quickly and inexpensively. These programs make it possible to have several hundred attendees live on the Webinar, and do a good job of handling registration to help you build your permission-based, opt-in list as your attendees register for the conference.

Some of the programs, such as GoToWebinar, integrate with Outlook's calendar and make it easy to send automated reminder e-mails. You can share control of the meeting with other presenters, mute attendees or enable live conversation, and have a simultaneous online chat to gather questions for a post-presentation Q&A session, or to allow presenter and facilitator to handle administrative issues live without interrupting the audio flow.

Other useful features to look for include the ability to do a quick, live poll of your audience to gather feedback or see where they stand on a particular issue or question. Some programs make it possible for participants to virtually "raise their hand" (identify that they want to ask a question) without a verbal interruption. Post-event surveys, follow-up e-mails, and event recording are some other features to consider. Some programs even integrate with Skype.

Online meetings focus more on collaboration tools, and expect that you'll have a smaller audience and less need for the administrative tasks that go into hosting a true online event. Fuze Meeting, GoToMeeting, MegaMeeting, Yuuguu, Microsoft Office Live, and Webex are popular programs for workgroups to meet, share desktops, collaborate on whiteboards or documents, and keep a virtual record of their meetings. A more limited but potentially effective way to do a small or ad hoc meeting would be to create a Skype conference call. Skype enables audio and video sharing, but lacks the collaboration tools of some of the other programs. That said, it's possible to collaborate via e-mail attachment or to use free programs such as FolderShare, Gubb, Zoho Planner, and Google Calendar. Alternatives to Skype for a video chat with a small number of users include Sightspeed and ooVoo.

If your idea of collaboration is more like Twitter for a private group, consider Co-op (coopapp.com), which is a private microblogging application (and at the time of this writing, free). On the other end of the spectrum, you can create a full-featured online classroom with an internal forum, the ability to share and post documents, and other features, with Moodle. If what you'd really like is a low-cost, simplified quasi-intranet, consider Qontext, a free tool that combines the ability to share files and see others' screens, with the ability to create groups and archive material. If your intent is to gather material from a large number of contributors, and confidentiality/privacy isn't a serious concern, you may be able to create what you need with free Wiki or Ning software. Google Docs is another free tool to store and share documents using the Google Cloud to archive your materials.

In fact, the down-and-dirty way to host a collaborative online meeting on the cheap would be either to use Skype or Google Voice, and then use tools from the Google suite of products to add the features you need, such as Google Talk (a version of instant messaging), Google Docs and Google Sites. It's proof that, whatever your budget, there's an online conferencing method out there for everyone.

Also, don't overlook what's available on LinkedIn through the site's applications. Huddle Workspaces is an app that provides you with an online private place in which to work and collaborate. When it comes to sharing your presentation, you can add DropBox, SlideShare, Google Presentations, or Portfolio Display to your profile to enable sharing. The Projects and Teamspaces app links your LinkedIn profile to a tool to help you keep track of your projects and other documents.

Teleseminars are different from conference calls because teleseminars often charge an attendance fee and usually involve a larger audience beyond a specific work team. A teleseminar is an online event, like a virtual speaking engagement or class, in which speaker and audience connect via a conference call. Attendance is usually managed by getting attendees to opt-in to a mailing list, which then shares the phone line and call password information via e-mail.

Teleseminars require less administration, because there is no visual component. To run a good teleseminar, you need a shared conference phone line and a way to record and share your call as Web-friendly audio. Sites such as FreeConferenceCall.com and

FreeConference.com make it easy to set up a call and offer the ability to host a large calling audience, in some cases up to 100 callers. Recording the calls, hosting on a toll-free line, and other extras are often available for added charges.

Most teleseminars don't bother with toll-free lines, given how prevalent cell phone plans with free long-distance calling have become. You'll want to record your teleseminars, so you can either pay the extra fee to the conference call site, or use a separate cloud-based service such as those offered by AudioAcrobat.com or InstantTeleseminar.com. These sites also charge a fee but provide many additional useful services. If you want to share visuals but don't want to bother with Webinar software, considering holding a teleseminar and sending attendees a link to handouts or to your slideshow so that they can follow along on their own.

Virtual meeting spaces can increase your ability to provide services to others and to collaborate with people who can provide valuable services to you. Marketing via teleseminars and Webinars can dramatically increase your branding and geographic reach. Best of all, many of the programs are free, and provide you global reach without leaving your office!

Results Reminder

!

How large could your business grow if you had no geographic boundaries?

Rule of 30

30

What are 30 topics you can envision either for online collaboration with your work team, or for sharing with prospects and clients via teleseminars and Webinars?

Action Items

1. Compare the cost of any live events that you're currently hosting (community education, prospect seminars) with the cost to produce them online as teleseminars and Webinars. Don't forget to factor in the cost of your time to commute to and from the venue and to set up and tear down.

2. Most professionals receive many invitations to teleseminars and Webinars hosted by other experts. Attend a few of these programs by leaders in your field and pay attention to how they are promoted and produced. What do you like? What would you avoid?

13
Sharing, Storing, and Safeguarding Documents

When you're on the go, or working on a project with clients and staff members who aren't in the same physical location, it can be difficult to make sure everyone is—literally—on the same page. Nothing takes a bite out of your productivity more than not being able to access the same version of a document, making changes to the wrong version, or having difficulty sharing the documents you've created or the changes you've made.

Fortunately, there are some easy-to-use solutions that are free or nearly free to help you share, store, and safeguard your documents, photos, and files. Whether you're working with a team of people or just want to keep your own projects organized, these programs can reduce wasted time, increase your on-the-go access, and give you peace of mind about the safety of your documents.

Content Management Keeps Changes Under Control

Whether you're working on a multi-media presentation, a manuscript, or a group project, it's important for everyone to have access to the most recent materials and be assured that they have the most recent version. Finding a simple way to record comments and track versions is essential, especially when several people must be polled for input and have their contributions incorporated into the final product.

"Content management" is the term that describes programs that help capture, track, and incorporate comments from multiple contributors. It's a fancy term that is the online equivalent of passing around a draft document to people who make corrections with different colored pens. Fortunately, several good content management solutions make it easy and affordable to gather input and incorporate changes from multiple people without making you pull out your hair.

If you use Microsoft Office, you've already got access to a powerful content management tool within Microsoft Word. The Track Changes feature lets you add to or delete content from a document and marks your alterations with underlining and strike-throughs. Different contributors' changes are marked with different colors. You can easily insert notes to ask questions, clarify why a change was made, or request input on alternatives.

If you save each marked-up version before accepting the changes, you'll have a history of what's been changed and who made the changes. That can be helpful if you later need to undo a change or don't remember who suggested a certain alteration. Just save the changed version, updating the file name to create a new version.

Office's Track Changes mode (under the Review tab), even eliminates the need to scroll down through the document looking for changes. You can use the Accept Changes button and choose the option to go to the next change, skipping over unchanged text. Or, if you've already read through the changes and agree, you can Accept All Changes and automatically incorporate all the revisions, removing the colored and underlined text. (Notes added in the sidebar will need to be removed individually.)

Office is a good general-purpose way to share and manage version control, but don't overlook Wordpress.com's built-in version-control management tools as well. For those who create significant amounts of content via their blogs, Wordpress has some nice version-control capabilities that come in handy when you're collaborating with co-bloggers or interrupted mid-revision.

If you're loading a lot of content onto your Website and revising or editing with a team of helpers, you may need to step up to more robust solutions. Adobe's Business Catalyst is a Website development tool with powerful content management tools built in. It's expensive compared to some other solutions, but then again, it's also more full-featured and comes with extensive support. Another option is Joomla, an open-source program that also makes it easier to manage, edit, and update all of your Website content. Box.com offers a business level of service at a very low monthly fee, which enables both document sharing and tracked version control for multiple collaborators. Once you know the extent of your content management needs, the level of technical sophistication that's right for you, and the money you're willing to invest, you can better compare and contrast these programs with others on the market. Many small businesses may never want or need a dedicated content management program, but it's good to know that such a thing exists in case you find your Website(s) growing beyond basic administration.

Beyond E-mail: Sharing Your Documents

E-mail is the workhorse for most document sharing. But what happens when you need to share a very large file? Many e-mail programs won't send very large attachments, and many Internet service providers won't allow extremely large attachments to be received. Public Wi-Fi speeds as well as connection rates and data usage charges for smartphones can also make it difficult (and expensive) to e-mail large documents. If your document sharing has outgrown e-mail, take heart: there are other options.

In the previous chapter, I talked about Moodle as a virtual meeting space. Moodle is a flexible, features-laden virtual place to meet, but it can also be used as a way to share documents among invited participants who have access to the secure virtual meeting space. As the Moodle organizer, you can post documents out in the virtual room, and participants can download them easily. Those with access to the "room" can upload their own documents, which others can access and share. Moodle includes a private forum board feature which makes it possible to discuss the shared documents and preserve discussions on a common theme (thread).

Four other popular document sharing services provide ways to upload large documents to a secure storage location and then share a link to the stored file, eliminating the need for massive attachments. YouSendIt.com provides online storage and also generates a link so you can share the document with others by allowing them to download it from YouSendIt. The basic level of service on YouSendIt is free as of the writing of this book, but plans with more storage and features are available for low monthly rates.

Box.com, Dropbox, and 4Shared are other options that provide both online storage and generate sharable links to stored documents. Each of the sites offers a free level of service, with more fully-featured levels available for monthly fees. Consider how your group needs to share and access files, because the features of the sites will appeal to different groups, so be sure to compare to find the service that is best for you.

When it comes to safeguarding your shared documents, be sure to read the fine print. Sites vary in their storage capacity, length of time stored files remain available, and level of protection. Be sure to note the security options available with each document sharing site to assure satisfaction and keep your files protected.

Results Reminder

!

Help your e-mails transmit more quickly and get fewer server-rejected messages by using links to share documents instead of attachments.

Rule of 30

30

Can you think of 30 documents you could be sharing via links instead of attachments?

Action Item

Compare the features, prices, and storage capacities of the sites listed here and consider your business's needs for content management and shared access. Be sure to think about tracking, restricted access, and security when comparing plans.

14
Where the Work Is: Virtual Freelancing Hotspots

According to tradition, legendary bank robber Willie Sutton was once asked why he robbed banks. "Because that's where the money is," Sutton is reported to have said.

"Sutton's Law" applies as well to finding virtual freelancing jobs. Why go to sites like Elance.com and Guru? Because that's where the jobs are—and where you'll find a diverse and remarkably skilled and affordable labor market to tackle your own overflow projects.

Not only do these online job marketplaces offer projects for self-employed specialists, but they're also a great place to find the extra help you need to grow your business on a project-by-project basis.

Connecting With Clients Across Town and Around the World

If your business lends itself to project work, consider creating a profile for your company on one or more of the virtual freelance sites such as Elance, Guru, ODesk, or Freelancer. (If you're in a more specialized field, such as software development, there are equally specialized freelance sites available too.)

Companies and solo professionals hire out through these sites for many reasons. Some make a dedicated commitment to bid daily on projects, understanding that competition is intense and that global competition favors low pricing. Other companies or individuals bid on projects in the hope of amassing a portfolio, updating skills, or landing larger, more lucrative assignments once they establish a relationship with an online client.

If you decide to throw your hat in the virtual ring, make sure to fill out your provider profile with complete information. Include a photo or logo, attach work samples and references, and spend some time developing short, concise proposals that you can mix and match as suitable jobs arise. You'll also need to fill out the information necessary for Elance and other sites to pay you and provide an end-of-year 1099 form (U.S. residents).

On virtual freelance sites, your track record of past projects is a visible form of credibility. Not only can prospective employers see how many jobs you've completed, but they can also see the ratings and comments posted by your clients. Needless to say, this makes customer service a top priority, and even then, some negative ratings are inevitable. Go the extra mile to make clients happy, but also develop a thick skin and realize that you won't be able to please everyone all of the time.

Elance and other online freelance sites support a level of global competition that makes it unlikely you'll win bids charging top dollar, especially without an online track record. Many employers hire from these sites looking for bargain prices and are able to hire the help they need because prices trend toward the low end of the spectrum. You may want to decide up front that you will only bid on certain types of projects that you can afford to do for a low introductory price. It's also important to realize that the sites do charge a "finder's fee" percentage to professionals to obtain projects through the site, and many sites require that future projects with the same employer be contracted through the job site for a certain length of time (meaning that repeat business will also be subject to the finder's fee percentage).

Virtual Assistance: Getting (and Affording) the Help You Need

In the early days of your business, like most entrepreneurs, you probably did everything: sales, Web design, research, and sweeping the floors. That's a fact of entrepreneurial life during a company's early days, but business owners who don't learn to delegate often find their companies unable to grow beyond what one person can handle.

Good help is affordable, especially when you hire the right skills on a per-project, as-needed basis. That's where online job marketplaces such as Elance, Guru, ODesk, Freelancer, and similar sites come in. Need a copywriter, graphic artist, or someone to help with administrative support? Think about the specific skills required, how many hours you would spend doing it yourself, and how much you're willing to pay to have someone do it for you, and then post your job through one of the job marketplace sites.

Within a few minutes to a few hours, you're likely to receive bids from professionals all over the world. Hourly rates tend to be incredibly competitive because of the global nature of the labor pool, and you'll find freelancers of all levels of experience offering their services. Read through the proposals carefully, narrow them down to the people who appear to be the best fit, and then go a step further to review your prospects' online portfolio or to interview them via e-mail or Skype.

In addition to helping you connect with professionals who can help you delegate essential tasks, sites such as Elance help you manage and track projects. Once a job is awarded to a freelancer on Elance, employer and freelancer have access to a secure project workroom where documents can be uploaded and downloaded, and comments and questions can be posted. Completed jobs can be paid for through Elance using PayPal, which shields the details of the employer's and freelancer's credit card or bank account data while enabling direct deposit of funds once a project is finished. Elance even generates 1099 tax forms for U.S. freelancers, making it easier for employers and freelancers alike. Pricing varies by site, but on Elance, it's free to hire. (Freelance workers pay a percentage to the site.)

With online job markets, it's easy to hire (and afford) the help you need on a one-time or repeat basis. The project format makes it non-threatening to try out a new freelancer, and easy to rehire professionals who have provided satisfactory performance. This provides the elasticity many small businesses need, giving them access to skilled help when the budget permits, without committing to a full-time or part-time employee they might not be able to afford on an ongoing basis. Online freelance sites also open up a pool of skilled labor unrestricted by geographic boundaries, making it more likely that you can find the right mix of skills and price to suit your needs.

Results Reminder

! The help you need to grow your business is more affordable than you might think! Check out the many talented professionals available through online freelancing sites.

Rule of 30

30

What tasks are you currently doing that could be delegated to someone else, enabling you to focus on more crucial work? Make a list of 30 projects, and put them in priority order.

Action Items

1. Check out the online freelance sites to see which might be the best fit for you, either as a service provider or as an employer seeking project help.

2. Look over the list of 30 delegate-able projects you compiled. Why not post your top priority project and see what happens?

15
Paying and Getting Paid

Paying for goods and services is a fact of business life. Getting paid is nice, especially when payments are made promptly. Whether you're sending or accepting payments, in today's e-commerce world, you'll need an easy-to-use, secure payment processor that fits the needs of your business. Fortunately, there are more options to choose from than ever before.

Consumer-Oriented Online Payment

There are a number of online payment services to choose from, but they differ in the details—and those details might be very important to you. If you're the one doing the shopping, decide whether you want to shop mainly by credit card, or whether you want the option of paying from your checking account.

If you are the one accepting payments, it helps to know how your customers prefer to shop. Do they prefer credit card transactions, or do they want to pay "cash" (instant transfer from their bank account)? As many consumers struggle to keep credit cards paid off and resist debt, more and more shoppers want to pay "cash" from a checking account.

PayPal is the granddaddy of do-it-yourself online payments. PayPal makes it easy for consumers to make online payments from a bank account or credit card, and for merchants to accept payments. One of PayPal's main selling points is its ability to protect sensitive information such as credit card numbers or bank account information. Regardless of whether you're the seller or the buyer, you only see the PayPal interface, never the actual account information from the other party.

PayPal also makes international buying simpler, with the ability to buy and sell in nearly 200 countries and currencies. Note that, while transactions can be processed in many non-U.S. countries and the money escrowed in PayPal, the process to withdraw funds varies by location.

Amazon WebPay (*payments.amazon.com*) leverages Amazon.com's internal payment processing capability to allow users to send or receive payments. As with PayPal and other online payment processing sites, both parties in the transaction must be registered with the service in order to fully complete the transaction. Amazon WebPay uses the payment information stored by the buyer/seller within their Amazon accounts to make or receive the payment. Amazon adds the additional convenience of having the option to load funds received onto an Amazon gift card, as well as being able to deposit to a bank account or use the funds within the Amazon WebPay system.

Many new players are emerging in the consumer transaction end of online payments, but it will take time to see if any gain the widespread acceptance and usage of the big players. Some of the larger banks have announced plans to create their own online payment network, but both parties in the transaction would have to have their bank accounts with one of the member banks, so at present, such programs lack the universality that PayPal and Amazon offer.

Both PayPal and Amazon have mobile phone apps, so consumers can utilize the services regardless of location.

Options When You're the Merchant

A growing number of Web-based payment services have sprung up to service the needs of online merchants. One of the ways these services differ from programs such as Amazon WebPay is that they serve the needs of the merchant to receive payments, but are not meant for consumer-to-consumer transactions. So where any individual can sign up for a PayPal account to shop, transfer funds to family members, or receive funds, online merchant-oriented services focus on the needs of businesses to send/receive money or complete transactions.

Intuit Payment Network is one of the better-known business-oriented online payment programs. Intuit Payment Network is integrated with Intuit's well-known Quickbooks program, making it easy to generate an invoice and record the online payment. Intuit Payment Network makes it easy to e-mail payment requests with a live link to the site and is designed to work well for links in e-commerce Websites.

With most online payment services, transactions are free for those sending money, but those receiving the funds pay a per-transaction fee. If you're considering using such a service (and to process online or phone transactions, you're going to need some kind of payment service), make sure to compare the terms of service, per-transaction fees, and contracts (if any) to make sure you choose the service that is best for you.

Accepting credit cards is a fact of modern business life, but how you accept them can be a sticky question, especially for small businesses or solo professionals who don't have a large volume of transactions. Traditional merchant accounts, available through banks, usually charge a monthly fee plus a per-transaction charge. That can be expensive, especially if you're a speaker, author, or other professional who accepts credit card payments on an occasional but not an everyday basis.

Several new online services have sprung up to make it easier than ever to accept credit cards without paying a monthly fee. Square was one of the first services to offer a free, mobile phone–based card scanner and drop monthly fees, charging only a per-transaction fee. Intuit's GoPayment also offers a free, phone-based card scanner and a similar no-monthly-fee structure. Neither service, at the time of this writing, requires ongoing contracts. Though the per-transaction fees can add up, pricing from Square and Intuit are more transparent than many bank-based merchant accounts. You know exactly what you're being charged for, which is directly related to the number and type of transaction. (There is a slightly higher per-transaction fee for keyed-in credit card information compared to a card swipe, because keyed-in information is deemed more risky.) PayPal's Merchant Services now allows you to accept credit cards even from non-PayPal members.

For those business owners who travel internationally, make sure your credit card service can function outside of the United States and accept cards from foreign banks. At the time of this writing, Square cannot process transactions beyond U.S. borders (although some merchants have reported success keying in Canadian card purchases once they return home to the States).

If your transaction volume begins to rise above the occasional, or you need more robust features, consider services such as Authorize.net and Paymate. These programs are probably overkill in terms of features and cost for a very small company, but as your need for credit card and online processing increases, you'll reach a break-even point where monthly fees become cheaper than per-transaction costs, and where you need more advanced merchant account services. Banks are gradually becoming more savvy entrants into this niche, so be sure to check out your bank's merchant accounts/online transaction processing, and compare and contrast to find the best value.

Being able to easily make and accept credit card and mobile payments is an essential step in growing your business. Online payment processing is also necessary if you plan to make sales via your Website or through sites like Ebay. Today's options are easier to use than ever before, both for buyers and sellers. Choose the program that best fits your needs and join the e-commerce revolution!

Results Reminder

!   To offer goods or services for sale via your Website, you'll need to be able to accept payments online. Otherwise, you're missing out on customers who will take their business elsewhere.

Rule of 30

30

Poll 30 of your customers or prospects to see what service they use for personal and business payment via the Web.

1. Compare your online payment options in light of your current sales volume. Which program makes the most sense when you factor in fees and the services your business needs?

2. Before you sign up for an online payment service, make sure that it will work with your Website or any online store in which you participate (Ebay, Amazon, and other online "mall" programs).

3. Pay attention to how a site handles key issues such as online data security and dispute resolution. Check out what end-of-year reporting is available to make tax time a little less stressful.

4. Make sure that the service you select can keep up with your travel by having the ability to process sales when you're out of the country.

16
Dashboards and One-Stop Timesavers

Sure, you'd love to rule the Web with a gazillion fans, friends, and followers on Facebook, Twitter, and other social media sites. You know you should be posting more frequently, if not once a day, at least several times a week. But who has time?

Fortunately for you, there are a growing number of social media productivity tools available to help you organize your online activity, making it easier for you to get more done in less time. Most of these sites enable you to post once and have your messages go to numerous social media sites, and a few of them have additional handy bells and whistles to help you manage your online life more efficiently.

The Magic of Dashboards

Dashboard programs provide all-in-one-place control, much like the dashboard of a car or airplane. Programs like HootSuite, Social Oomph, Ping, and TweetDeck make it possible for you to plan your social media campaigns and load content in advance.

One of the central benefits of a dashboard program is the "set it and forget it" feature: the ability to enter content into the dashboard and schedule blog posts, Facebook updates, and Twitter Tweets to go out over a period of time. While pre-scheduled content is no substitute for live conversations, dashboard programs fill the very real need of making sure that busy people maintain a baseline, consistent level of content without large gaps. You can always pop in online to add updates, post photos, or jump into conversations, in addition to your pre-scheduled content, but you won't get to Thursday and realize you haven't posted or Tweeted all week.

A caveat: many dashboard programs post content with a source credit that says "from API," meaning that it has been automatically posted. Some social media users and search engines view pre-scheduled content as less desirable than live-posted information, regardless of the quality of the actual information itself. This means that to keep your friends, fans, and followers happy and to raise your social media score with ranking programs such as Klout and Alexa, keep a good balance of live posts and pre-scheduled posts. On the other hand, realize that pre-scheduled content is better than no content. Followers, search engines, and ranking programs also take a dim view of prolonged absences. I maintain that if the best you can do during a busy period is pre-scheduled content, being present on a consistent basis far outweighs the alternatives.

HootSuite is one of the best-known dashboard programs. It's a powerful, user-friendly site that offers levels of membership ranging from a basic free service to a more robust Pro level. The heart of HootSuite is the ability to enter posts in advance into the dashboard and program when your content goes live across multiple social media sites. This works especially well if you are using a virtual assistant to help you load the content you've written, and it makes it easy to keep track of what you've said and where you said it.

For those who want to go deeper, HootSuite also has the capability to do detailed tracking across your sites, looking at follower growth, metrics from Google Analytics, and other indicators. For larger organizations with a social media response team, HootSuite not only prepares reports, but enables team collaboration and the ability to assign messages to team members for follow-up. Other features, such as file upload, follower management capabilities, and localization are great for enterprise-level use, but not important for the average small business or solo professional user. HootSuite also has a convenient mobile app for smartphones, so you can keep an eye on your account when you're on the go.

SocialOomph, the program formerly known as TweetLater, is another dashboard with many of the same capabilities as HootSuite. As you'd expect, SocialOomph lets you pre-load and schedule on Twitter, blogs, and Facebook, and provides both a basic free level of service and an extended professional level. You can track keywords, view your @Mentions and Retweets, purge spammy Direct Messages (DM), and monitor multiple accounts from one dashboard. The professional level offers blog integration, profile filters, and some interesting ways to assess which of your followers might be your most valuable prospects. While SocialOomph leans heavily toward Twitter with a nod toward Facebook and blogs, it does enable Ping to send your information to LinkedIn and MySpace.

TweetDeck is another of the well-known dashboards. TweetDeck offers connectivity with Twitter, LinkedIn, Facebook, and Foursquare. It makes it easy to create and manage Twitter Lists and helps cut down on Twitter spam. Another valuable feature is the ability to follow Twitter Trends, real-time topics, and TwitScoop to stay abreast of the most popular topics. TweetDeck is available for iPhone, Android, iPad, and a new Web-based interface, as well as the original desktop version. At the time of this writing, TweetDeck is free, which is good for a solid, basic dashboard. However, if you're looking for a pro version with additional features or you want more analytics, at the moment, they're not built into TweetDeck, so one of the other dashboards may do a better job if those elements are important to you.

Customized Dashboards for Specific Requirements

Beyond the main benefits of a social media dashboard (pre-posting, scheduled content, analytics, and so on), several other programs are out there for social media users with more specialized needs. These dashboards may not be useful for everyone, but they do fill specific needs, and it can be good to know they're out there, just in case you need what they provide.

Threadsy gives you a way to combine social media with your e-mail, and connects with many of the major social media networks. If you'd rather have a single dashboard active rather than switching between different screens, Threadsy is worth a look.

If multiple people in your organization are maintaining your social media presence, you can bring sanity to the situation with MediaFunnel. MediaFunnel lets you assign different roles to those in your social media team, consolidates log-in information, and helps you monitor your brand and important keywords. It incorporates some of the features of HootSuite and the other basic dashboards, such as pre-scheduling Tweets and posts, and assigning messages to team members to handle questions or issues. MediaFunnel also has a mobile capability, as well as a built-in URL shortener to make it easier to Tweet links. MediaFunnel offers a basic free level for small organizations, and a fee-based level for larger companies.

MarketMeSuite is yet another all-in-one free dashboard with the ability to manage multiple profiles, pre-schedule content updates, access the program from a mobile phone, and post through Ping. In addition, MarketMeSuite has a location-targeted capability and interfaces with Klout and PeerIndex to help you determine your online popularity. MarketMeSuite offers the ability to monitor branding across your platforms and supports use by a team of users. The location targeting is a nice feature, since it can help you augment your social media connections with real life meetings, or help a local business focus its messaging on locally based followers.

Regardless of which dashboard program you use, remember that it's your content that matters. If you're creating content that is highly targeted and meets the needs of your ideal audience, how it gets posted is a back-office issue of no consequence to your online network. Remember also that while these dashboards have the ability to increase your reach, poor quality content will hurt your brand, and over-posting with hard-sell copy will lose you friends and followers, and may get your account suspended. These are power tools; use them with caution!

Results Reminder

!

Plan one day a month to compose your content, then use a dashboard to schedule and post it.

Rule of 30

30

Try creating a themed sequence of 30 posts or Tweets, one for each day of the month. Pick a different theme each month, and use them as the jumping-off point for your online conversations.

Action Items

1. Most of the dashboard programs mentioned are free, and those that aren't have a free trial period. Explore the sites and try out the one that seems like the best fit for your needs.

2. Pay attention to the content you receive from others, especially from people who are bigger-name thought leaders. Can you tell from their posts whether or not they are loading content with a dashboard? Does that affect how you feel about the content?

17
Empowering the Road Warrior

Whether you're a true road warrior or you just seem to be on the go all the time, mobile apps on your tablet PC or smartphone can make your life much more productive. Even better: many great apps are free, and others are very inexpensive, so productivity seems sweeter than ever.

What are the basics you need to get work done when you're not in the office? At a minimum, you need some good ways to take notes, work on or read documents, store and retrieve files, and access the tools you usually have close at hand in an office or on your laptop. Fortunately, there are apps for all these needs, and on your smartphone or tablet PC, they're truly at your fingertips.

Managing Your Documents When You're on the Road

Smartphones and tablet PCs are desirable because they're smaller and lighter than a laptop, and easier to carry around. But that same portability comes with a price: they can't carry all of the files stored so conveniently on your laptop. Good news: an ever-increasing array of apps bridge that gap between laptop and mobile device, making it easier than ever to work on the go.

Quick note-taking is essential to keep your thoughts organized, especially when you're constantly in motion. iPhones and iPads come with a basic Notes app, which while not perfect, is quite suitable for the kinds of things you'd jot on a cocktail napkin. Though it doesn't sync with other apps and it doesn't have any security beyond that of your phone's keypad, Notes is perfect for jotting down something you don't want to forget and assuring that you won't lose the scrap of paper you wrote it on. Not perfect, but it's free, and there's a lot of basic function that goes a long way.

Evernote also has a mobile app, so if you love it on your other devices, you can bring it along in your pocket with your phone or tablet PC. A few other note-taking apps, including Awesome Note, WriteRoom, Simplenote, and RememberTheMilk, make it easy to jot down what you need to remember, and come with varying additional capabilities, such as being able to sync to other devices or store data in the cloud.

Pages is a very good, basic app for reading and writing documents. Documents you create in Pages can be e-mailed in RTF or Word format, and you can e-mail yourself small documents in those formats and edit using Pages. Though I find it cumbersome to type documents of any length with the on-screen keyboard on a phone or tablet PC, when you pair Pages with a wireless keyboard, the result is pretty efficient.

For those who want to access their Microsoft Office files from their iPad or iPhone, Quickoffice Pro HD bridges the gap between Microsoft and Apple. There's also a scaled down version, Quickoffice Connect Suite. With Quickoffice, you can open a Word document, access a PowerPoint presentation, or edit, save, and share other types of Office-based files. Office2 HD is a similar program, offering a few more capabilities for word processing than some of the more basic apps. Documents To Go Premium Office Suite not only handles Word and PowerPoint, but it will also access Excel spreadsheets, and it syncs with storage programs including Dropbox, SugarSync, and Box.net.

Storing and Retrieving Files

Remember those cloud-based storage programs I told you about earlier in the book? Most of them have mobile apps, so you can access your information no matter where you are or what kind of device you're using.

This is where the power of the cloud really makes a difference, because through cloud-based storage, you can access, edit, and share many more documents than your mobile phone or tablet PC could store locally, without slowing down your device or maxing out your storage. Google Docs, SugarSync, Box.net, and Dropbox all have mobile apps, making it easy to grab your documents no matter where you are.

Many apps also allow you to e-mail documents as attachments, which is a nice backup storage option. Be wary, however, of relying on e-mail if your document is large or your Wi-Fi connection is of questionable strength. Remember, too, that if you're using a public Wi-Fi connection in a hotel or airport, your data is not encrypted, so don't e-mail or upload sensitive files until you have a secure connection. Also, mobile plans differ in the way they charge for data usage, especially if you're using your own Internet hot spot, so make sure you understand your phone plan pricing or you could be in for a surprise when your next bill arrives.

Online Office Essentials

When you're working on the go, many of the helpful tools you take for granted in your office aren't at hand. Fortunately, there's an app for that.

Appzilla and Appzilla2 are the Swiss Army knives of the app world. Appzilla comes with 90 mini apps, and Appzilla2 has 120, including a book lamp, checklist, countdown timer, area code look-up, alarm clock, currency converter, date calculator, flashlight, and links to nine Google apps. Sure, Appzilla also has fun things like a metronome, moon calculator, and Morse code generator, but those can be a momentary distraction when you're stuck in an airport.

Need a dictionary? Try the Dictionary! app or the Dictionary.com app and have the English language at your fingertips. The Dictionary.com app even includes a thesaurus, or you can grab FreeSaurus on iTunes.

Looking for a phone number? Before you pay for a 411 look-up, try the WhitePagesMobile app. Use it to search for either businesses or people, and get maps or directions. YPMobile gives you the Yellow Pages business directory, plus ratings and event information.

Want to translate a phrase into Chinese or Serbian? The FreeTranslator app will help you with the important short sentences necessary to get by when you're traveling. Can't remember the source of a quote? Quotationary probably has what you're looking for. Need to know where in the world you are? Try World Atlas HD for maps and useful details about every country on the globe. Struggling with a metric conversion question? Convertbot has the answer. Not sure when your package will arrive? DeliveryStatus will get an answer for you. Need a mirror to see if the lettuce from your salad at lunch is still in your teeth? The Mirror app turns your smartphone into, yep, a mirror that you won't lose in your desk drawer.

If you miss your filing drawer back at the office, try FilesToGo, a cloud-based filing system that gives you access when you're traveling. No need to juggle loose printouts on the plane: GoodReader can translate a PDF file into an iPad-friendly format so you can read it from your touchscreen. Bento is an app that works like a virtual clipboard/database/desktop organizer for either the iPad or iPhone.

When you'd rather speak than use a keyboard, you've got several great options. DragonDictation's app (and program for the PC) lets you speak into your smartphone and activate your e-mail or your text messages. To use your phone to take dictation or just record a message to send later, try Say It & Mail It Pro Recorder or QuickVoice2TextEmail.

Keep track of your time while you're on the road with TimeMaster + Billing—it's even got a billing module. Take your pick: Timewerks, TimeLogger, or iTimeSheetLite can also help you manage and monetize your time. They differ in capabilities, so pick the one that works best for you.

If there's still anything you're missing from your brick-and-mortar office, a quick search on iTunes or Android app store will probably turn up several contenders to help you create your home away from home.

Results Reminder

!

What tasks do you find the most difficult to do remotely when you're on the road? There's probably an app for that!

Rule of 30

30

What are the 30 documents or programs you use the most? That's where you're losing time when you're out of the office without an online alternative.

Action Item

Think of the tasks you routinely need to complete when you're out of the office, and look for cloud-based programs and/or apps to make your life easier.

18
Smartphone and Tablet Apps for Busy People

Just because you're out of the office doesn't mean your productivity can come to a standstill. While you can't have your laptop with you everywhere you go, smartphones and tablet PCs make it possible to do all kinds of tasks that once required a full office setup.

Many of the cloud-based programs discussed earlier in the book have smartphone and tablet PC apps so that you can use those same programs when you're not at your desktop. In addition, many social media sites also have mobile apps, making it possible for you to keep working your online marketing strategy when you're on the go. In addition, other apps just make it easier to have the tools you need at your fingertips, conveniently stored inside your mobile device.

Mobile Versions Connect With the Cloud

Need something from your desktop when you're in the car? GoToMyPC has a mobile app to make it easy for you to retrieve whatever you need. Likewise, mobile devices with

Internet access can connect with your cloud-based storage programs such as Box.net, Dropbox, and Google Docs so that you don't need to wait until you are in your hotel room or at a temporary office to get the information you want.

Opening, reading, or editing PDF files can pose a problem when you're away from your fully loaded desktop computer. If your work entails being able to review PDF documents, consider PDF Reader. This app lets you open PDFs from your iPhone as well as make editing changes, such as strike-outs, highlights, or underlines, and save your edited file.

Use PDF Converter or PDF-it if you want to save an Office file into PDF format. PDF Expert bundles the reading and editing capabilities together, along with the ability to sign your own signature to PDF documents and fill out PDF forms. If you want to share your PDF-based presentation, consider PDF Presenter (for iPad), which offers easy-to-use fingertip controls to flip through your slides.

For those who live or die by delivery schedules, you can track your FedEx parcels with the FedEx Mobile app. Breathlessly awaiting a snail mail delivery? USPS Mobile not only lets you track and confirm package delivery, it also includes a handy way to find your nearest post office, look up zip codes, schedule a pick-up, scan labels or calculate shipping prices. Not to be outdone, the UPS Mobile app lets you do most of the same tasks that the USPS app permits, only with a UPS focus.

Social Media Apps Make It Easy to Maximize "Power Surges"

Many business people lament that they don't have time for social media. Yet a growing number of customers have made it clear that they prefer to interact with businesses via social media, so you are notable by your absence if you aren't part of the online conversation.

Here's another way to think about the social media/time dilemma. Do you ever have short periods of downtime, such as arriving early for an appointment, waiting in an airport, or cooling your heels awaiting your child's dismissal from soccer practice? If so, mobile apps make it possible for you to tackle your social media outreach in strategic "power surges."

First, make sure you've loaded the mobile apps for Facebook, Twitter, and LinkedIn to your smartphone or tablet PC. Once you've got the apps loaded, sign in to your accounts so that they will automatically connect you in the future. Now you're ready to hop online whenever you have a few extra minutes and leverage the power of social media.

Connectivity is only part of the story, however. You need to have a plan for what you'll do after you connect. As I discuss in my book *30 Days to Social Media Success*, you'll get the most impact for your effort if you create a list of at least 30 short, strategically focused actions that you can take in 15–30 minutes. You can keep your list on a note-taking app on your mobile device. If you're pressed for time, use 10- or 15-minute "power surges" to get the same amount of work done in short bursts. Here are some ideas:

~ "Friend" two or three new people through your personal profile and suggest they "like" your business fan page.

~ Connect with two to four people who already "like" your fan page to start up a conversation.

~ Comment on posts or reply to comments on your pages.

~ Send a couple of Tweets, upload a photo, or link to an article that would be of interest to your audience.

~ Use your smartphone video camera to record a short tip and upload it to YouTube.

~ Check in with at least two of your LinkedIn connections—congratulate them on recent career news, introduce them to some of your other connections, or ask how the family is doing.

~ Make a LinkedIn recommendation or ask for a referral.

~ Check in with your Facebook or LinkedIn groups to comment on a current topic, offer an answer to a question, or help out a fellow group member.

~ Reply to a Direct Message (DM) on Twitter, Retweet a good Tweet from someone you follow, or do an @ name public reply to a comment of interest to your followers.

Social media is designed for short attention spans, so it's perfect for you to jump on and jump off when you're on the go and your time is limited. You may find that accessing social media through your mobile devices makes your wait time fly and actually makes you look forward to connecting online!

Your On-the-Road Toolbox

You never know what might come up when you're away from the office. Here's a rundown of some other helpful mobile app tools to keep your workday humming along.

~ MyToolbox turns your smartphone into a setsquare, bubble level, and caliper—just in case you have a handyman moment when you're on the go.

~ MultiMeasures gives you a timer, stopwatch, ruler, plumb bob, protractor—even a seismometer—all in your smartphone.

~ DocumentsToGo lets you access, edit and save your Microsoft Word documents (including formatting) as well as sync to your desktop.

~ Want to keep tabs on your money? Take a look at a consolidated tracking app such as Mint, which can track your investment, and bank account balances, help you budget, and alert you to overdraft risk.

~ Need a better way to scan cards, receipts, or other documents? CamScanner converts your smartphone to a scanner.

~ If you're on the road and looking for the best local deal on gas, try GasBuddy.com to find the cheapest fill-up in your neighborhood or anywhere in the United States or Canada.

~ Most road warriors accumulate many restaurant, hotel, and other frequent shopper cards. Who has room in the carry-on bag for all that? CardStar stores all of your loyalty cards on your smartphone so that you get your discounts without bulking up your wallet.

Your goal is to find the apps and Websites that help you be as comfortable and productive as possible when you're away from the office. Explore, experiment, and enjoy!

Results Reminder

!

Don't just focus on productivity when you're busy—also look for ways to decrease stress!

Rule of 30

30

What are three things each day that you can do in 10 minutes or less to increase your visibility, improve your productivity, or enhance your connections?

Action Item

Keep a log for one week of all the things you need or use when you're out of the office. Then check to see if there is a mobile app to solve that problem while eliminating the need to carry extra bulk (such as manual calendars, discount cards, and so on).

19
Mobile Apps for When You're on the Road

Travel is a fact of life for most business owners. Whether you're traveling by plane, train, or automobile, you need access to information to help you get where you're going.

I've covered many cloud-based services and mobile apps to keep you working when you're out of the office. That's a good start—but it doesn't cover everything you need to know in order to remain productive on the go. Some of the most valuable information a traveler needs is about travel itself—weather conditions, road and airline delays, and other data that can make or break your day. Fortunately, there are a growing number of programs to help you avoid schedule-busting problems, and in this chapter, I'm going to introduce you to some of them.

Traveling Essentials

If you skipped any of the previous chapters on storing and retrieving files from the cloud, accessing your desktop PC remotely, or collaborating remotely, now is a good time to go back and get caught up. For people who spend a good bit of time on the road, these programs and apps aren't just nifty tools; they're lifesaving essentials.

A growing number of businesses use QR (Quick Response) codes to share information. You'll find them on posters, boarding pass printouts, business cards, menus, and seemingly everywhere else. A QR code is a pixilated box designed to be read by a smartphone. Once a smartphone scans the QR code, the user is taken directly to a Website, social media page, or other online destination, usually one offering some kind of special or coupon. QR HD is one of many smartphone apps to consider to make sure you're not missing out on great deals and extra information.

FlightAware is a free app to track delays, cancellations, and gate changes. FlightBoard isn't free, but it has the capability to show you arrival and departure information for any airport worldwide. FlightTrack is another option, giving you real-time information on departures, delays, gates, and other key information.

Like most travelers, you probably use a packing list to make sure you have all your essentials. You can use some of the list apps discussed earlier in the book, such as Notes or Remember The Milk, or download Packing (+TO DO) or uPackingList to make sure you never forget your socks or flash drive again.

TripIt is a travel organizer app that syncs with your e-mail to gather all your travel confirmations into one convenient place. The MyTravel app in LinkedIn is by TripIt. MyTravel shows you where your LinkedIn connections are traveling and shares your itinerary with them, so you can maximize your "serendipitous" connections when you are on the go.

For travels that cross time zones, consider TheWorldClock app. It's not free, but it could keep you from accidentally calling home in the middle of the night. While you're at it, check out WorldExplorer. Again, it's not free, but it's like having a travel guide in your phone, with plenty of maps, articles, and ratings so that you can get the most out of your compressed sightseeing.

Finding free Wi-Fi when you're away from home can be a real hassle. Fortunately, there's Wi-FiFinder, an app that scans the area around your location to let you know where to find the nearest paid and free Wi-Fi spots.

Don't overlook Foursquare if you're a creature of habit when you travel. If you return to the same cities and same places over and over, Foursquare helps you get credit for loyalty, and lets your friends in that location know where to find you. Google Goggles is a fun app that lets you take a picture of a landmark near your location with the camera on your smartphone and get back both an address and a list of nearby resources. And if you're lost inside an airport, try Point Inside Shopping & Travel for maps of airports, malls, museums, and theme parks, plus coupons and special offers while you're there.

Weather can play havoc with a trip. The Weather Channel app can help you know what to pack and whether or not you'll need a coat (or umbrella). For a more fanciful approach, try iDress for Weather, which gives you temperature and precipitation information plus icons to tell you which clothes to pack. If you're worried about major storms, RadarScope is a paid app that turns your smartphone into a meteorologist's weather map—rather helpful if you're in a hurricane-prone airport.

Comfort and Relaxation

Part of being productive includes knowing how to unwind after a long day. Here are some apps to help you pass the time on a long flight or help you settle in once you get back to your hotel.

Ambiance lets you record your own soothing sounds or lets you pick one of the more than 2,000 free ones on the list to help you relax. You can also upload your own relaxing playlist to any tablet PC with music capabilities.

With airline restrictions becoming tighter and tighter on baggage space, now just might be the time to switch to e-books. Kobo, Nook, and Kindle all have apps for smartphones and tablet PCs that give you an essentially unlimited library at your fingertips. Megareader gives you access to the many free public domain books available for download, including classics by some of literature's most famous authors.

Prefer a movie? You can purchase and store movies and TV shows to your tablet PC or smartphone from iTunes. Or, watch what's available on Hulu, YouTube, or Netflix on their mobile or tablet apps (but make sure you have free Wi-Fi or are sure of how your data plan charges for streaming video).

If you spend time walking around unfamiliar cities, consider EveryTrail and City Walks. EveryTrail includes GPS information, live street mapping, and a compass, plus other useful information. City Walks is like having a tour guide in your pocket, chock full of interesting information about local sights, history, and colorful details. Google Earth is another good option, as is MapsWithMe.

If you like to eat, you'll love UrbanSpoon. Enter the name of the city where you're looking for a restaurant, and you'll see a list of local eateries, plus customer comments and ratings. No longer will you be resigned to eating in a chain restaurant because you don't want to take a risk on an unknown local place. Add your own comments when your meal is done and help guide the next traveler! AroundMe is another app for finding not just restaurants, but all kinds of places that are close to your current location. Yelp combines GPS, search, maps, and ratings to help you choose where to go or what to do. TripAdvisor is both a Website and a mobile app that shares travel information, customer ratings, and useful forums. For purists, the mobile version of the venerable Zagat guide isn't cheap, but it is available for smartphones and iPad.

Wherever you roam, make sure you take your smartphone or tablet PC, and load up on free and inexpensive apps before you leave home to make your travel and downtime more productive and enjoyable!

Results Reminder

!

When you're looking at apps and cloud programs, think about how to get more from your free time as well as your time on the job.

Rule of 30

30

Where do you travel most often? Think about your 30 top business and pleasure destinations, and look for apps to help you make the most of your visits, both on and off the clock.

Action Items

1. Use MyTravel on LinkedIn to see where the people in your network go most often. Can you pick up tips on conferences or industry events that you might not have known about?

2. You can get double or triple the benefit from your travel time if you arrange early morning or after-hours meetings with other people from your network when you're in their hometown. Who would you benefit from networking with, and when will you be in their neighborhood?

20
More Tools for Social Media Productivity and Presentations

Virtual productivity isn't just about apps and gadgets, although it may sometimes seem that way. It's what you do with the apps and gadgets, how you schedule your time, and how you manage your attitude that really matters.

Productivity Starts With Your Plan

You'll get the most bang for your buck on productivity by using that plan I talked about at the beginning of the book. Take a look at your calendar a month in advance, and determine what part of your plan you want to accomplish in the next 30 days. Break it into daily doses, and pay special attention to what activities work best with the other things on your schedule.

For example, if you're heading out on a flight, take a list of quick phone calls to make while you're waiting at the gate. Airport Wi-Fi is iffy, so why not knock off a bunch of calls while you wait, then do Wi-Fi-based tasks from the quiet of your hotel room instead of trying to balance your laptop on your knees in the terminal?

Find yourself with time on your hands and no Wi-Fi? You could reply to e-mails (to send them later when you have a connection) without the interruption of new mail coming in. Got Wi-Fi but not a lot of time? Ten minutes is all you need to post to Facebook, send a Tweet, or update your status line on LinkedIn. Or, check in on Foursquare and see if anyone you know is hanging out near the airport Starbucks.

Use your smartphone or tablet PC notepad to keep your daily to-do list in front of you. I load Word or PDF files into Pages or iBooks to read on the plane when I don't have Wi-Fi. I'll also send myself documents and PowerPoint presentations via e-mail, which I download and open from my iPad or iPhone before getting on the plane. That way I can read or edit them without being connected.

Always have a back-up plan of what you could do if your initial plan goes awry. That means having a variety of types of tasks on your to-do list, and a flexible mental attitude that can shift gears depending on the situation. All that matters is that you get through the list by the end of the day; the order of what you do doesn't matter.

Expand Both Your Reach and Your Productivity

If you're like most business owners, you need enhanced productivity when it comes to expanding your influence. That means reaching more people with a persuasive message in a shorter amount of time and, preferably, at low cost. Fortunately, these apps make it easy.

Bloggers take note—Triberr.com could be for you. Triberr is an invitation-only blogging community that helps you reach more people through the power of collaboration. As a Triberr member, you can join the "tribes" of other bloggers in complementary specialties that are likely to have readers who would be interested in related content. When you join someone else's tribe, your blog posts are automatically Tweeted to your partner's Twitter feed, and their blog posts are automatically Tweeted to yours. Some people consider that a tremendous advantage, while others prefer links that are personally Retweeted. The verdict is still out on whether audiences will feel served or spammed, but if you have a clear niche and not too many tribe members, it could work for you. The site has tribal membership limits and other rules to keep users from spoiling the system, and it's worth checking out.

Ever feel inundated with your Twitter and Facebook inbox? Check out Refynr.com. Refynr lends itself to business use of Twitter and Facebook, because it helps you filter out "interruption" notices such as FourSquare or Facebook games. You can choose which topics/keywords to follow or block, and it works on laptops, smartphones, and iPads. If you need to be able to jump on and off social media and find the valuable messages right away, take a look at Refynr.

If you add value to your Twitter and Facebook posts by sharing content from other sites that could be of interest to your followers, explore Bufferapp.com. Bufferapp makes it easier to collect interesting content as you come upon it and then share it at times that are convenient to your readers. So if you browse the Web at 2 a.m., sharing interesting news articles as you see them may mean your readers never get the links because they're asleep. On the other hand, it's a hassle to bookmark everything and try to come back to it later. Bufferapp handles that for you. It's new and still evolving, but worth exploring, especially given the value of sharing reposted links.

Another tool to overcome social media overload is FriendFeed. FriendFeed creates a dashboard to monitor updates from blogs, social bookmarking sites, and social networking sites. The program makes it easier to read and share from anywhere, including e-mail or smartphones.

SocialMention.com bills itself as a tool "like Google Alerts but for social media." I couldn't have said it better. You get daily e-mails alerting you to whatever you've entered as relevant for SocialMention to monitor, but it won't be looking at the whole Web, just social media feeds. Not only is this a good tool to scope out the competition, but it's a way to track what key contacts are doing so that you can be Johnny-on-the-spot with congratulations or relevant e-mails.

While we're talking about productivity, don't overlook social bookmarking sites such as Digg, Delicious, and StumbleUpon. These sites work like the online equivalent of the break room bulletin board, where coworkers tack up interesting articles with a sticky note that says, "Read this!" Digg and the other sites work the same way, only in cyberspace. When you find an interesting article, you can share it with the whole world, not just your network, by posting it to one of the social bookmarking sites.

Ideally, you want your own blog posts and online articles to be so useful that others will post them to share with the world. It's considered bad form to bookmark your own stuff, but there's no rule against having your virtual assistant do it for you! Social bookmarking sites operate on the principle that good stuff will rise to the top of the lists. You can use them to increase your online productivity by scanning these sites to see what the hot topics, big headlines, and trends are, and to see what content your fellow netizens consider to be valuable.

Presentation Productivity

If you need the ability to do one-on-one presentations on the go but don't always have a laptop with you, take a look at Keynote. Keynote works a lot like PowerPoint, but for iPad, iPhone, or iPod touch.

You can create and share a slideshow with text or photos, which makes it pretty handy. Hooked on PowerPoint? Slideshark for iPad makes it possible to view PowerPoint slideshows on the iPad, and it can be connected to a VGA projector to share with a larger audiences. At this time, however, you can't originate a PowerPoint presentation in Slideshark, so you have to upload one you've already created.

Another option is to save your PowerPoint as photos (remember the photo sharing sites earlier in the book) or as a PDF. Or upload your slideshow to one of the cloud storage sites and download it via your tablet PC Web browser to share it in that format.

Apple seems to understand that iPad users want to be able to share what's on their device with at least a small crowd. The Apple TV service ties into the iCloud, and, when coupled with the AirPlay wireless device, makes it possible to project what's on your iPad onto a high-definition TV. The Apple Digital AV Adapter is another option, with the convenience of having your iPad screen mirror what's on the big screen. For those who need to project onto a big screen, there are a growing number of pocket-sized (or nearly so) LCD-type projectors that work with tablet PCs. Box.net also has an adapter to connect your iPad to a VGA projector. This enables you to access a presentation stored on Box.net through your iPad and project it for the room.

You can be sure that options will grow for online filtering and presentations as users recognize the benefit. Keep an eye out for new entrants and updates: change is the only constant on the Internet!

Results Reminder

!

Laptops slow down passage through airport security, but iPads and similar devices don't have to be taken out of your bag. Save yourself time at check-in by traveling with your iPad instead of your laptop.

Rule of 30

30

What are 30 tasks from your daily routine that you could do with the apps and programs in this chapter to make your life a little easier?

Action Item

What do you need to access via your tablet PC that would enable you to leave your laptop at home when you travel? Find the apps to make that happen, and lighten your backpack!

21
Expanding Your Contacts

Productivity leaps forward when you go from one-to-one communication to one-to-many. That's the genius behind social media, online PR, and the programs and apps that help you connect with groups of people all over the world. At the same time, we all hunger for one-on-one interaction, which remains at the heart of business development and successful marketing. While the traditional ways of personal networking remain viable, today's fast-paced world makes it difficult to fit in time for many luncheons, breakfasts, early coffees, after-work mixers, or evening business events. Fortunately, our wired world has created new ways to have the high-touch of personal networking with the efficiency of the Internet.

Keeping Your Contacts Warm

You know the difference between a "warm" lead and a "cold" call: a lead is "warm" when there's a recent personal connection, and "cold" when it's a total stranger or the connection is long dormant. In our busy, mobile lives, it's all too easy for business friends, colleagues, coworkers, and others to slip from day-to-day, in-person connections to "whatever happened to?" status. People move, change jobs, drop out of associations, or change their daily routine, and suddenly that "warm" connection has grown cool.

LinkedIn is your number-one online tool for warming up those long-lost connections. LinkedIn is a different kind of social network from Facebook and Twitter, and that difference makes it very valuable. Whereas the value on Facebook and Twitter lies in the ability to meet many new people, LinkedIn's value comes from deepening relationships with people you already know. In fact, trying to connect with people you don't know on LinkedIn could get you bounced from the site, because the emphasis is not (initially) on meeting strangers but on rekindling friendships with people from your past business life who have slipped away.

To get the most out of LinkedIn, make sure your profile is filled out completely. Start with a current business headshot of yourself. Then fill out your past positions so that your former colleagues from throughout your career can find you by searching on company names. The same thing is true for alumni networks: they tend to be very active, and people will search by alma mater and graduation year.

LinkedIn gives you the ability to recommend people who are connected to you. This is a powerful way to strengthen your connections. You want to recommend people whose work you can attest to as being of high quality. Odds are, people you recommend will then recommend you in turn. You may also find that someone you know makes the first move and recommends you; if you can legitimately do so, it's considered polite to return the favor. Having recommendations on your profile makes for a more complete picture and helps to integrate you into the LinkedIn community.

Be sure you also list your relevant business Websites on your LinkedIn profile: your primary business site, your business blog or podcast, and your Facebook and Twitter pages. If you have awards, certifications, or publications, LinkedIn has added sections to include those, as well. You're not bragging; you're making it easier for people to find you by including more searchable terms.

On LinkedIn, go through your Rolodex, business card files, e-mail address book, or old contact lists, and look for the coworkers, vendors, suppliers, bosses, subordinates, colleagues, and others who you've known throughout your career. Send them an invitation to connect with you, but be careful to only choose people who are likely to immediately remember your name. Otherwise, too many people indicating that you've tried to connect with them and they don't know you could get you in trouble with the system.

Broaden your search to the neighbors, relatives, and non-work connections who might be a valuable part of your business-related network. LinkedIn isn't the place for personal socializing, but it has a social side, much like a chamber of commerce mixer. Be sure to only add people who will honor the business focus of LinkedIn, and keep the others on Facebook.

One of LinkedIn's most valuable features is its ability to show you the people to whom your connections are connected. These "degrees of separation" can prompt you to invite people you already know whom you had forgotten. Even more powerfully, you can find out when someone you want to meet already has a connection to someone you already know. Just as in the real world, that's when you ask your friend for an introduction. This is another reason why you want to make sure all your LinkedIn connections are "real." You'll be more comfortable asking, and your contacts will be more comfortable making the introduction if they actually know you.

Your status bar gives you the chance to make Twitter-like one-line updates. This is a great way to let your network know what you're doing, to ask a question, or to see if anyone can recommend a resource. You'll also see the status updates of the people in your network, so be as helpful as possible when they post a question, or cheer them on when they announce a success.

LinkedIn also has groups on every topic, as well as alumni groups for universities and many large companies. When you become involved with a group, you have the opportunity to deepen your relationships and meet people to whom you're not already connected. Always be helpful, stay on topic, and don't sell. Instead, be a good neighbor by answering questions, offering ideas, suggesting resources, and lending a hand whenever possible.

Your Summary is where you can share your value proposition, or your Transformational Value. Don't just say what you do—tell readers what benefit and outcome you create for your clients. While this isn't a place to do a hard sell, you can help readers connect the dots to see the value you provide, identify your target audience and ideal clients, and let readers know the kind of people and organizations from whom it would be most valuable for you to gain a referral.

In other chapters, I've mentioned some of the many helpful LinkedIn apps. These only work, of course, if you have a profile on LinkedIn!

Networking Beyond LinkedIn

While LinkedIn is the centerpiece of online networking, it's not the only valuable site. Gist is a cloud program that consolidates all of your contacts and lets you access them from any of your mobile devices. Even more valuable, Gist consolidates the news about your contacts, including their social media posts and online mentions, and serves it up in an easy-to-read dashboard. It's like having Google Alerts set for your entire network of contacts. This can be especially helpful if you are always looking for a reason to make a phone call or send an e-mail—now you can easily comment, congratulate, or check in, based on your contacts' most recent online mentions.

Foursquare makes it possible for you to let your friends know where you are and what you're doing. In addition to its ability to provide coupons and discounts for the retail and restaurant locations you frequent most often, it's also a way to take the "chance" out of chance encounters. No more relying on luck to run into people you know at the diner, coffee shop, or grocery store; now you can tell them where you are and invite them to join you.

Plaxo is an online address book that helps you manage your contacts. If you have the problem of having contacts spread across phone lists, e-mail addresses, social media sites, and other devices, Plaxo might be what you need to bring everything together into one cloud-based address book. Plaxo also helps to keep your contacts current by looking for potentially outdated information and e-mailing contacts asking them to update their information.

Other ways to manage your contact list includes Google Contacts, which integrates with your other Google accounts, and Highrise (Highrisehq.com), which goes beyond being a simple address book to being a central repository for notes, follow-ups, and reminders, verging on a true contact management system. It's both a cloud-based program and a smartphone app.

If you collect a lot of business cards, consider a card reader app. BusinessCardReader uses your phone's camera to scan a card and enters the information into your phone's address book and/or LinkedIn. The BizSnap app not only scans business cards, but it can also scan receipts. WorldCard Mobile is another choice for easy card scanning and uploading.

Extending and managing your personal network doesn't have to be difficult. Use the power of social media and smartphone apps to make sure that none of your contacts ever go cold again.

Results Reminder

! The warmer your contacts, the more valuable your network.

Rule of 30

30

Reach out to at least one contact every day for a month and see how your opportunities expand.

Action Items

1. Make a list of all the places you have separate contact lists. What would be the value to you of having that information centralized and available to you everywhere?

2. If you're not already on LinkedIn, or your profile isn't complete, make it a priority to get out there and start connecting.

22
Organizing Time and Thoughts

When you're in constant motion, it can be difficult to keep track of your time. It can also be a challenge to keep your mind focused on the ideas and strategies important to your business.

Thanks to a growing array of time and thought-organizing programs and apps, you have more options than ever before to keep your schedule on track and capture those brainstorms when they occur.

It's About Time

If you track your time, either for billable hours or to monitor your own productivity, it helps to have an easy-to-use tracking program. Toggl works with both mobile and desktop devices to keep your own online timesheet. Even better, it integrates with Basecamp, Quickbooks, and Freshbooks to translate your time into billable hours, and it can handle multiple rates by client or team member, as well as different currencies. Toggle also can give you reports and graphic summaries to show you where your time is being spent. It's scalable for teams of up to 200 people.

Log into Tickspot.com and you can manage your time by client and project. You can create a time budget for each task, and see how you're doing against the budget.

Elance has a time-tracking option that enables employers to get a more detailed view of how their virtual providers are spending their time. Providers also have the ability to upload status reports that can range in detail from short recaps to more complete time tracking.

Other options include Easy Time Sheet, which can track time, hourly rate, and notes. It might be just what you need if you aren't heavily dependent on tracking multiple jobs. ClockedIn is another app that not only manages projects, but it can help you stay on task for your personal goals as well. Timely.is takes an incentive approach and lets you know how much you've earned as you complete your project. It takes the "time is money" approach to a new motivational level. Timely works for groups as well as individuals, and can also handle non-billable projects.

Keeping Your Thoughts Straight

Mind-mapping is a technique that allows users to capture their thoughts and place them in a spoke-and-wheel graphic that shows how each concept relates to other concepts on a topic. If you're a big fan of mind-mapping, check out SimpleMind+, a smartphone app that makes it easy to create and store mind maps on your iPhone, iPod Touch, or iPad.

OmniGraffle is another mobile app that supports mind mapping and a whole lot more. It not only helps you diagram, but it can do 3D shapes, a variety of fonts, and supports freehand drawing. When you're done, you can share your creative vision with teammates via PDF.

For the verbally inclined, Dragon Dictation, which I've discussed previously, is another way to capture thoughts on the go. The app is a modern twist on familiar technology, making any smartphone a voice recorder. Dragon not only captures your voice, but it also converts the spoken word into text or e-mail.

iPro Recorder records your voice, and it records in enough clarity that you can use it to create Web audio and podcast interviews. Recorder is another iPhone app that makes it easy to speak your mind and remember later what you were thinking about.

If your goal is not just to save your recording on your smartphone but to send it via e-mail, Note2Self has what you're looking for. iRecorder and YouNote are two other low-priced apps that provide no-frills basic recording. YouNote also lets you send drawings, typed notes, or photos, as well as recordings, making it a little more versatile than the voice-only recorders.

Your time is precious, so tracking it makes sense when you're out of the office. Brilliant ideas can slip away if you don't grab them right away. Those are two good reasons to consider using apps and cloud programs to manage both time and thoughts.

Results Reminder

! If you waste precious minutes looking for loose papers on which you've tracked ideas or billable hours, increase your productivity and gain back time in your day.

Rule of 30

30

Do you spend 30 minutes or more tracking time or writing notes to yourself? Using these apps to save just 15 minutes a day could save you 91 hours over the course of a year!

Action Items

1. Pay attention to the system that comes most naturally to you to track your hours or organize your thoughts. You'll get better results if you find an app that matches your personal style, instead of trying to change your style to suit the app.

2. When you begin using a new app, give yourself some time to adapt. Even an app that matches your style will take some time to get used to.

23
Promotional Tools on Facebook and Twitter

Growing your business productively means understanding all of the tools available to you. Just as smartphones and tablet PCs have redefined productivity on the go, social media has redefined how people communicate and, more specifically, how consumers want to communicate with businesses.

Facebook, Twitter, and LinkedIn are the three major social media platforms. I've already talked in depth about LinkedIn, but it's worth taking some time to look at how Facebook and Twitter can help promote your company while boosting your productivity.

Facebook Basics for Business

As of the writing of this book, Facebook was approaching one billion users. While Facebook was originally designed as a recreational site to connect with friends, businesses were quick to see the potential. In fact, businesses have embraced Facebook faster than the Facebook architecture has adapted, leaving Facebook often scrambling to catch up to how its subscribers want to use the site.

Being present on social media for a company today is much like being present on the Web: you are judged negatively if you're not there. Just as many consumers would not consider a company to be a "real" business without a Website, so many purchasers look for a Facebook presence to see if you are "real." What matters is that consumers have decided that they want to have a two-way conversation with the companies they patronize, and firms that abstain from being part of the dialog do so at their peril.

At the very least, you need to have a Facebook Business Page. As Facebook has adapted to the needs of business users, these Business Pages have become easier to create and use. Facebook wants businesses to promote from a Business Page and not from a personal profile. Ignoring this rule can get your page deleted from Facebook.

A Business Page works a little differently from a personal profile page in that a Business Page can't "friend" individual users. Instead, users are invited to "like" the page and thereby opt-in to receive automatic updates whenever the page adds new information.

Today's consumers value a connection through Facebook because they want to be able to express their opinions, ask questions, and feel as though they are being heard. They want to do business with people, not faceless corporations. Companies that learn to listen can reap valuable benefits, from uncovering (and being able to fix) customer service issues, to discovering competitive advantages when a rival firm has dropped the ball, to new product ideas gleaned from the suggestions of loyal purchasers.

When you create your Business Page, make sure both your logo and your photo are prominently displayed. People need to find you as a business, but they want to connect with you as the person behind the business. Fill in the Information section, making sure your content is all about the benefit you provide to your customers and what you do for them (not just a laundry list of products and services). Include your other Websites, links to blogs and podcasts, and business contact information, so your Facebook fans can find you on the Internet.

If you already have a profile page, Facebook wants you to use it primarily for personal/recreational content. However, it's okay to talk about business some of the time, just as you would in real life. Also, with a profile you can invite people to "like" your Business Page, and suggest that your "friends" also visit your Business Page. Just keep your profile mostly personal, to remain compliant with Facebook's Terms of Service.

Content is essential for attracting and keeping readers. Ask questions that are business related, provide tips, and post links to interesting and helpful videos, articles, and blogs, even to content that you didn't create but that your audience would appreciate. Repurpose articles and answers into Frequently Asked Questions and use other information you've written into short, helpful, one-paragraph snippets of content.

Try to keep a conversational tone. Don't use a hard sell, and don't constantly promote. Instead, draw your readers in with open-ended questions and try to get them into a dialogue. Facebook users want to connect with the person behind the business, so keep the conversation "business casual," as you would at a networking luncheon. That means that it's okay to talk a little bit about superficial personal subjects, such as your pets, vacation highlights, sports teams, and so on. Always make sure that the information you share shows you in an ethical, trustworthy light. Be human, but also be professional! You can also reward those who "like" your page with occasional special discounts and coupons.

Promote your Facebook Business Page at every opportunity. Put a "badge" (Facebook can generate this for free) showing your Business Page icon on your business Website. Add the address for your Business Page to your business cards, signage, invoices, handouts, and all marketing material (Facebook makes it easy to create a short, readable page address). Where your Website is a one-way conversation (you speaking to your customers), view your Facebook page as the opportunity to learn from having a two-way conversation with your prospects and buyers.

Facebook also offers the ability to place ads that show up on the profiles of other Facebook users who fit the demographic description you provide. You set the budget and the duration for the ads, and a campaign costing just a few hundred dollars can lead to hundreds of thousands of impressions and hundreds of clicks. This is a great way to drive traffic to your Business Page or to your company's Website.

Facebook has tightened up its rules for allowing contests, but that doesn't mean that contests are out of reach for small businesses. PinpointSocial.com specializes in template-driven, do-it-yourself Facebook campaigns that comply with Facebook's rules but are easy and affordable for small businesses to run. Used in conjunction with Facebook ads, this is a great way to increase the "likes" for your page, essentially increasing your Facebook opt-in. Constant Contact has also added a social media tool that creates Facebook landing pages using templates, with the advantage that the tool also integrates with Constant Contact's impressive e-mail marketing capabilities.

You can also add value to your Facebook Business Page through extra add-on applications within Facebook. For example, one app allows your blog to automatically post to your Facebook page (RSS or Really Simple Syndication), increasing your productivity by getting additional exposure for each blog post. The same is also possible for your Twitter or podcast feed. For companies that sell on eBay, Facebook has an app that interfaces with your eBay site. Apps change frequently, so be sure to look for the ones that would be right for your business.

I've already told you about many of the dashboard programs, like HootSuite and SocialOomph, which make it easy for you to schedule content and keep a consistent presence. It's also worth taking a look at MarketMeSuite, which combines the benefit of a scheduling dashboard with several nice marketing tools.

The Promotional Productivity of Twitter

If you're a person of few words, you'll admire the elegance of the idea behind Twitter; each post is just 140 characters. That's about two sentences to get your idea across. What can you do in two sentences? You'd be surprised.

Twitter is a great place to share links to valuable content (you can shorten them to preserve more of your character limit by using a site like Bitly.com or TinyURL.com): videos, interesting articles on other sites, blog posts, audio, or downloads. Find an article of interest to your audience? Share the link, and then Tweet a few thoughts and ask a question to get a conversation going.

What else can you talk about in 140 characters? Recommend a business book and say how it influenced you. If you were at an event and saw a speaker who talked about something useful for your readers, Tweet about it! You could even include a link to the event Website, speaker's home page, or to a video or blog post related to the event. Or share a motivational quote, comment on a business-related topic that is in the news, or let readers know if you have an upcoming promotion or special event.

As with Facebook, you can reward the people who follow your page with periodic links to free downloadable material of value to their business, or give them sneak previews of special prices before you post the specials on your Website. People who follow you can ask you questions, either publicly or privately, so you'll want to monitor these so you can answer promptly. (Several of the dashboards make this easier.)

Twitter is also a great way to give live updates from the business-related events you attend. If you're at a conference, either as a speaker or an attendee, send periodic Tweets about what you've liked, what insights you've gained, what well-known experts you've heard or met, and other information that gives your followers a you-were-there feeling.

Whenever you use a keyword in your tweets (such as the name of an event, a book, a celebrity/authority, or product), make it searchable by putting a hashtag (#) in front of it. For example, if you are talking about the book *Think And Grow Rich*, you would Tweet #ThinkAndGrowRich. That way your Tweet will show up if anyone searches on the name of the book. You can also see what topics are popular by searching Twitter's Trending Topics. Chiming in on a hot topic (if it relates to your business) can draw attention to your Twitter page and help you gain more readers.

Promote your Twitter page in all the same ways I suggested for your Facebook page, and make sure you let people know what's in it for them to follow you. Tell them what kind of helpful content you post, and if you provide discounts or coupons, let them know. You can also have your Twitter feed automatically update your other online pages, such as your LinkedIn page or Website, by using RSS. LinkedIn has a free RSS application, and your Web designer can add it easily to your home page.

Remember that the biggest key to productivity on social media is keeping your top goal firmly in mind and approaching your online time with an action list. Go onto Facebook or Twitter with one to three tasks that can be accomplished in 10 to 30 minutes, and keep your mind on business while you're there. By using this "power surge" process, you accomplish more in less time and avoid distractions during working hours.

What can you do in such a short time? You can invite people to become your friend or "like" your page, ask a question or make a comment to someone who is already a friend or who has "liked" your page, post a quote or short tip, or check out what top speakers and experts are posting on their sites. You can post a link to a helpful article or set up a Facebook ad. You'll be amazed what you can get done in a short period of time when you keep your activity focused on achieving your top goal and reaching your ideal audience.

Results Reminder

! Your customers who use Facebook have made clear how they want to communicate. Put yourself where they are for best results.

Rule of 30

30

What are 30 short tidbits, tips, quotes, or special deals you could create especially for your Facebook fans?

Action Items

1. Get over your Facebook fears by spending a day compiling your content for the month, just to prove to yourself that you can do it. Decide on themes, and then have some fun. It's not difficult or scary—just do it!

2. Consider using Facebook fan-gates (contests that encourage newcomers to "like" your page) to increase the number of fans who will receive all of your updates automatically.

24
Promote With Online Reviews and Directories

Productivity is all about getting more results from the time or money invested. Promotion is one of the areas where businesses look to increase their productivity—in other words, to get more bang for their buck. Online reviews and directories are two more tools businesses can use to get their name out in front of more potential consumers and reach them *during* their decision process, when prospects are actively planning a purchase.

The New Directories and the Power of Word of Mouth

Many people remember when there was only one directory: the phone book. As a growing number of consumers migrate to cell phones instead of land lines, phone books have become less valuable, both to businesses looking to be found in their pages, and to telemarketers using them as a way to cold call. But with the rise of the Internet, a new breed of directory has taken hold, a hybrid of the old phone book category listing crossed with a dynamic, interactive social media tool with which consumers can provide feedback to merchants and communicate among themselves.

Yelp, Yahoo! Local, and Citysearch are three of the most popular online directories. They include a wide variety of business types, ranging from products to services to hospitality/entertainment, combining basic information, such as company name, address, and phone number, with the option for customers to add comments. The company information may have been added by a consumer or by the company itself. Categories are rarely an exhaustive listing of every business in that type (but then again, the old phone directories only included companies willing to pay for an ad).

Most directory sites create their basic content in two ways: collecting publicly available information from other published sources, and allowing users to add sites live online. This means that your business may already be out there, so it's a good reason to Google your company on a regular basis to see where you're showing up and to make sure that your basic information (address, contact information, category) is correct. You may have also been added by a recent customer, or by a helpful person who knew about your firm and wanted to make the listing more complete. You can also add your own company, and there are some strong reasons why you should consider doing so, if you're not already out there.

The first reason for making sure you're represented in online directories has to do with consumers' preferences. Today's consumers turn to online sources for information gathering far more often than they pick up a printed directory of any kind. Online information is believed to be more accurate because it can be updated more frequently than a printed document. Obviously, this isn't always the case (incorrect information can be posted just as easily as accurate information, and sites don't always get updated as frequently as they should be). In general, though, consumers have had good luck finding the information they're looking for online, so they come back again when they need to search for something else. Most directories for the general public (that is, not a membership directory for an organization) list companies for free, because they want users to add content. If your company isn't in the directory, consumers in a hurry may not bother to look further, and you lose out.

The second reason for being in online directories is word of mouth. Consumers have always trusted what other consumers say about a business more than they trust paid advertising. Before the Internet, those conversations took place over the backyard fence, in the line at the grocery store, or at social events. Now, consumers like to read reviews posted by other customers before making a choice to buy. They're not only interested in the quality of the product; they also want to know about the quality of the customer service provided by the merchant.

The third reason for being in online directories is search-ability. Every time your company appears online, it helps to boost your search engine results. The more people are talking about your company and the more places it appears online, the higher the search engines place it in their results pages. Being present online pays off, not just in being visible on an individual directory site, but also through the secondary boost every online mention gives to your Google results.

The idea of customers posting reviews for the world to see makes a lot of business owners nervous. While they believe in the quality of their product and service, they fear that competitors or mean-spirited people may post unfair or inaccurate information online that could damage their business. It's certainly possible that despite sterling quality, a disgruntled person might post a negative review. However, according to Yelp's own analytics, the vast majority of reviews posted are very positive. Most people posting reviews want to alert readers to their favorites, not trash companies.

What if someone does post a negative review? If you find a negative post online, take a deep breath and let yourself calm down, then read it again to see if there is any truth to the customer's disappointment. Business owners can post replies to reviews, but you should do so carefully and strategically to avoid making a bad situation worse. If the customer had a bad experience, you can make a public apology, offer them a replacement, and try to make it right.

You may not sway the unhappy person's opinion, but you've publicly demonstrated that you heard, you listened, and you attempted to correct the situation. Most consumers realize that mistakes happen; they just want to know that you care enough to fix it. You may not win back the disgruntled consumer, but you'll go a long way toward preventing one comment from souring the opinions of others.

If the comment is minor, saying nothing may be the best way to handle it. If the customer didn't like the seasoning in your soup, for example, you probably can't change their opinion without changing your recipe. People are entitled to their opinions, so if it's a matter of taste and not quality, readers will probably take it for what it's worth and make their own judgment. By replying or trying to argue with the consumer, you just draw attention to the post, turning a minor comment into a major argument and making yourself look argumentative.

What if someone posts a really bad comment? If the comment is abusive or uses vulgarities, racist language, or profanity, it's likely that you can appeal to the site owners to have the comment removed. Many sites include internal filters to remove over-the-top comments or push them far down in the results, making it less likely that an outrageous comment is seen. It is also possible to contact the user who posted the comment and politely ask him or her to remove it. If that doesn't work, and the comment is truly both malicious and defamatory, it is possible to bring legal action. How far you take it depends on just how much damage you believe the comment can cause. Another way to deal with negative comments is to ask your loyal customers to help you out by posting their own positive comments, which will push an unreasonable review so far down the queue that it will be seen by fewer people. And you can ask your friends to also request that a truly objectionable review be removed (sites may pay more attention to multiple user requests).

In my experience, companies worry far too much about the possibility of negative comments. Does your company operate in an ethical manner? Do you offer a quality product that lives up to your claims? Do you strive for good customer service and follow through on your promises? If so, there should few reasons for your customers to say anything bad, and many for them to sing your praises. Here's something else to consider: consumers have talked about businesses to their friends and neighbors since the beginning of commerce. With today's online directories, you now have a chance to hear what they're saying, and if the comments reveal areas for improvement, you can make the changes necessary to avoid future problems. View comments as feedback, and recognize that it's impossible to make everyone happy. The positives of visibility and good user comments far outweigh the negatives.

The Power of Online Reviews

While directories such as Yelp permit customers to add comments, there are also plenty of other sites that specialize in reviews. These include dedicated review sites like ConsumerReports. org, which covers a wide array of consumer products, and more specialized sites reviewing movies, books, camera equipment, and other niche interests. As newspapers and magazines have cut "soft" news, such as reviews, online sites have sprung up to fill the gap. Some of these sites, such as RogerEbert.com, are from a well-known expert (in this case, Chicago Sun Times long-time movie reviewer Roger Ebert), but many are written by citizen-journalists out of a passion for the subject.

Love reading? You can start with reviews posted by readers on Amazon.com, and even read best-of lists compiled by other Amazon users. But if you want to go deeper, you'll find dozens—perhaps hundreds—of blogs and review sites in your favorite genre or non-fiction topic dedicated to book reviews. In many cases, the reviews are the opinion of the site owner and will be colored by their personal likes and dislikes (which is part of the charm for readers). In other cases, the review site will recruit reviewers who agree to submit reviews according to the site's guidelines.

You'll find review sites for cameras, camping equipment, board games, computer peripherals, video games, luggage, sound equipment—just about every interest under the sun. Some sites have only a few hundred readers, but more established sites can get millions of hits from a legion of dedicated readers who turn there first for information. So, how do you get included?

Begin by reading the site carefully. Many sites explain how they acquire the items they review. In some cases, reviewers speak solely from their own experience with items they buy and use themselves (you'll find this true for many book review sites, for example). Other sites have a policy for receiving free samples from companies, and will disclose that the items were sent free of charge instead of purchased. Big review sites (such as ConsumerReports.org) have a budget to purchase items for review, to avoid any appearance of conflict of interest.

Next, read the reviews to determine the personality of the reviewer. Some reviewers try hard to be impartial, citing both the positives and negatives. Others enjoy trashing everything or take a very snarky tone. That's part of their personality and it draws their loyal readers, but it may not be a good fit for your product. Know what you're getting into before you try to place your product with a reviewer.

Follow the site's guidelines for requesting a product review. They may want you to query first before sending the actual item. Some sites will review certain types of products only on a seasonal basis, or may have designated months for different categories of items. If so, their guidelines will tell you how far in advance to submit your request and/or items to be considered for a review.

Should you only shoot for reviews from large sites? Not necessarily. Smaller sites, blogs, and social media review pages may not have millions of readers, but they probably do have a loyal core of followers who could be valuable early adopters and spark buzz. These sites are usually more approachable than some of the very large review pages, and may provide quicker turnaround. Treat every reviewer with respect regardless of the size of his or her following, and be sure to follow their guidelines to the letter.

Realize that when you submit your product for review, you agree to accept whatever they post. Reviewers are not required to like your product just because you sent it to them for free. Even a positive review may include some criticism just to be balanced. It's also possible that a reviewer may write a negative review, especially when the review is highly subjective, such as reviews on books, restaurants, food items, and other products dependent on the user's tastes. You can't demand that a negative review be withdrawn unless it is truly vulgar and profane or meets the legal definition of libel, which can be difficult to apply given the protection afforded to journalists, even for unpopular comments. Where user comments on a directory might be removed by the site administrators, when you're dealing with a review site, you're usually dealing with the owner whose "product" is the site's opinion. That's why it's so important to assess the personality of a reviewer before submitting items for review.

Getting a great review online can provide tremendous visibility to consumers who might not otherwise have become aware of your product or service. Excerpts from great reviews can also be quoted in praise of your product, and links to positive reviews can be posted on your site. (Never copy significant portions of a review without the writer's permission, since reviews have copyright protection.) While there is some time and effort involved in compiling a list of relevant reviewers and sending off items for review, you can receive tremendous promotional value for a relatively small investment in time and shipping costs—a truly productive way to market your company!

Results Reminder

! Consumers turn to the comments of other users and to review sites to explore options and validate their own opinions.

Rule of 30

30

Reviews and directories are included in the 30 touches required to turn window-shoppers into buyers.

Action Items

1. Explore the online directories such as Yelp, Yahoo! Local, and other sites. Is your company already listed? Is the listing accurate? Has anyone posted comments?

2. Compile a list of reviewers who cover your type of product. Read their guidelines and make sure the sites are a good fit for their tone and perspective, then begin querying the best options and get your products reviewed!

25
Online Reputation Management

Productivity takes a hit if you have to spend time cleaning up a mess. The bigger the mess, the more time gets wasted on clean-up. Needless to say, preventing or containing messes can boost productivity and give you peace of mind, which enables you to keep your focus on your top priorities.

That's why it's so important to know what's being said about you and your company online, and who's saying it. "Reputation management" refers to being aware of what is being said about you online so that you can work to remove inaccurate or defamatory content, respond to legitimate complaints, and capture positive comments and testimonials. The term can also refer to techniques to reduce the impact of unfavorable content via search engine optimization techniques.

Let's be clear: if you've done something unethical or have shoddy business practices, you're better off cleaning up your act and making restitution than trying to suppress legitimate negative comments. And, as discussed in Chapter 24 in regard to online directories, other people have a right to their opinions and to speaking those opinions online. They aren't required to like your products, and they may say so publicly. Reputation management should never be seen as a way to cover up bad business practices.

That said, it is important to understand how you and your company are viewed in the marketplace so that you can make course corrections as needed and reap the benefits of glowing reviews. And, inevitably, incorrect information will make its way online, so it's also important to have a way to become aware of erroneous content and straighten out misunderstandings. We perform all of these tasks daily in the real world without really thinking about it. Reputation management is just the online equivalent of staying plugged into the grapevine to see what others are saying.

Reputation Management Basics

You've created an online presence for yourself via your Website, Facebook and LinkedIn pages, blog, Twitter feed, and other Internet activity. This presence becomes part of your personal and professional branding, which is why it's so important that everything you post online be consistent with the professional image you want to project. Yet at the same time, other people are free to tag you in photos, mention you in their blogs and Facebook posts, refer to your company and products in articles and reviews, or Retweet your Twitter content. You control what you post yourself, but how can you possibly track everything posted by others, including people you've never met?

Google Alerts is a first line of defense. It's a free tool that enables you to track keywords any time they show up on the Internet, and those keywords should include your name, company name, and product names. Anytime your keywords are used, Google Alerts sends you a report which includes a link so you can see for yourself. It's not perfect; I've found it to work well for content on blogs and Websites, and less so for content on Facebook and other social media sites, but it still snags a tremendous amount of information and is useful as a basic reputation management tool.

SocialMention.com, which I talked about in the dashboard chapter, is also valuable as a reputation management tool. SocialMention fills the holes left by Google Alerts by focusing specifically on social media and covers an impressive variety of site types. While no program will capture everything, Google Alerts and SocialMention used together should give you a very comprehensive picture of what the market is saying about you (and how much they're talking about you).

If you've been online very long, you've discovered that many people have a name that is the same or very similar to yours (and perhaps to your company or products). One way inaccurate information finds its way into the Internet data stream is via mistaken or confused identity. Most of the time, these mistakes are honestly made, and can be cleared up with an e-mail or a clarifying post. If you find that you're frequently being confused with a particular person or company, you may want to add a note in your Frequently Asked Questions (FAQ) stating who you're not.

People in the public eye (which includes prominent businesspeople as well as writers, speakers, and educators) may sometimes be the victim of pranksters who set up unauthorized sites to detour legitimate Web traffic, make a negative statement, or just cause havoc. This is especially easy to do in social media, and the result can be a site purporting to be written by you that is making statements you would never make, statements that could be damaging to your brand and reputation.

One way to assure that people are finding the real you is to use a site such as Zoolit.com, which provides a landing page that shares all your sites: social media, Websites, blogs, and so on. Using a landing page such as Zoolit enables you to give readers a way to verify whether or not a site that purports to be from you really is yours.

Hands-On Reputation Management

I've talked about the networking value of recommendations on LinkedIn. Gathering online recommendations via LinkedIn is also a way to solidify your online branding and actively manage your reputation. Don't be shy about asking former coworkers, bosses, colleagues, and clients to provide a recommendation if you had a positive working experience with them. That's part of the LinkedIn culture. You'll want to make sure you have plenty of recommendations for your current role, but you may want to also actively seek out recommendations for prior roles to bolster your credibility and show the depth of your expertise.

Naymz is similar in some ways to LinkedIn (extensive profile, forums, online networking), but it goes further to help you actively manage your brand and reputation. Naymz has what it calls a "RepScore Ecosystem," in which you aren't just asking for a recommendation from former colleagues and clients; you're asking for them to provide anonymous feedback on your honesty and ethics. Naymz also has its own "Reputation Monitor" to provide you with yet another stream of information regarding what's been said about you online. Naymz also lets you know when your profile has been visited, although it does not tell you who checked you out.

What happens when a negative comment is posted on a ratings site and you can't get it removed or retracted, but it's not serious enough to sue for defamation? One tactic is to make the comment more difficult to find by increasing the searchability of other, more positive content. The Internet favors recent and highly targeted information, rewarding it by pushing it to the top of the search results. This pushes older content off the first pages of results, and few searchers bother to go more than one or two pages deep.

How do you do this? One tactic is to ask your clients and professional friends to add ratings of their own (you don't have to disclose the reason behind your timing for the request). You can spiff up your Search Engine Optimization (SEO) on your most relevant sites, such as your home page and your blog, assuring that they jump to the top of the search results. Or, you can hire a PR agency or reputation management firm to make positive posts on your behalf on a large enough number of sites that the sheer volume of new positive mentions pushes old copy off the first page of search results.

Use this last tactic (hired guns) with caution. Mobilizing actual clients, friends, and even family to post genuine testimonials or positive reviews is still authentic and organic, even if you reminded them to do so. (Never offer rewards in exchange for positive comments.) Hiring people to manufacture testimonials is unethical, and you'll be found out eventually, which will send your online reputation plummeting. If you do decide to use a publicist, a better tactic would be to post a wealth of factual, positive information (such as verifiable high satisfaction ratings or award announcements) or repeat testimonials or positive reviews from legitimate clients and reviewers. Just creating a blizzard of new, positive, highly relevant, and keyword-optimized informative posts can go far to push down a negative review.

Yet another reputation management tactic involves making it difficult for anyone to create a profile or Website using your name or products by claiming them yourself. Some people make it a practice to buy up all of the domain names available for their own name or their products, such as the .biz, .tv and other domain suffixes. This keeps cyber-squatters from purchasing these domains and attempting to sell them back to you later at an inflated cost, or using them to create fake sites purporting to be from you. If you consider this tactic, remember that you'll have to pay domain registration fees annually, so buying up dozens of URLs that you never intend to use can get expensive.

If you don't have the time to actively monitor and manage your reputation, there are companies that will do it for you. Some of these specialize in particular industries, such as hospitality or construction, while others serve a variety of business types. Services range from monitoring and reporting to assistance in handling complaints or dealing with malicious comments. Fees vary according to the services provided. If you decide to use a monitoring and response agency, do your homework before making a commitment, and check out the reputation of the company online before hiring them to work on your behalf. Some reputation management companies have been caught using unethical strong-arm techniques against people who have posted legitimate complaints that were well within their constitutional rights. There's a big difference between hiring someone to help you keep an eye on what's being said and employing cyber goons to intimidate or harass consumers who have merely stated their opinions. The best way to protect your online reputation is to always deal ethically, both online and offline. Keep your word, don't overly hype your products, and deliver what you promise. If something goes wrong, do everything you can to make the situation right. You're far better off putting effort into delighting customers and running a clean operation than investing resources into cleaning up avoidable messes or attempting a cover-up. Nothing stays hidden for long in today's online society. Honesty and vigilance are your best online reputation management tools.

Results Reminder

At a minimum, set Google Alerts to see what's being said about you and your competitors.

Rule of 30

30

Who are 30 former clients, vendors, colleagues, subordinates or bosses you might contact for LinkedIn recommendations, online reviews, or testimonials?

Action Items

1. Check out the reputation management sites listed in this chapter. Even if you decide against going deeper than Google Alerts at this time, you may find the sites useful in the future.

2. Google yourself and see what comes up. You may be surprised! Now set Google Alerts, and you'll be notified when new information crops up.

26
Online Event Promotion and Management

If you hold live or online events, you know that productivity and efficiency makes the difference between a successful event and a dud. Back-office processing is often the hidden factor that makes or breaks an event. That includes event promotion as well as the mechanics of selling tickets, processing payments, collecting attendee information, and managing sales data.

I've already talked about tools for creating teleseminars and Webinars, but online event promotion and management includes much more. Whether your event is live or online, you can increase your productivity, help your event run more smoothly, and improve attendee satisfaction by making use of cloud-based event management tools—many of which are free!

Live or Virtual?

A few chapters back, I talked about the online tools available to create teleseminars and Webinars. Those are the two basic types of online events, but you can use those basic formats to create events as simple as a one-hour phone call, or as complicated as a multi-day online summit or virtual tradeshow.

The visible components of live events are complex enough: arranging for a meeting venue, handling catering and hotel services, setting up audio/video, managing traffic flow, and processing sign-in or on-site payment efficiently. But the back-office component is just as complex: managing registration, tracking attendees, collecting relevant attendee opt-in and preference information, creating and distributing materials, securely handling and tracking payments, and promoting the event both online and offline.

Most business owners have attended basic teleseminars, comprised of a conference call and, often, downloadable handout material. These calls can be a one-time call or part of a call series. Webinars add the ability to see a slide presentation in real time, or to incorporate video or a shared whiteboard or desktop. While the use of technology simplifies some of the logistics regarding venue, travel, parking, and catering, the need still remains for promotion, back-office processing, and secure handling of registration data and payments. Trade shows, expos, career fairs, and other festivals heighten the complexity by the sheer number of vendors, the space and services requirements, and the three-ring circus nature of having multiple programming tracks, vendor areas, and display space.

Before you make the decision about whether your event should be live or virtual, realize that many events today are a hybrid of the two formats. Holding a live event and streaming video of the presentations to people who choose to attend virtually can increase your audience, making it possible for people to attend from across the country or around the world. Using the techniques covered in the virtual meeting space chapter, you can create private breakout sessions, schedule interviews or one-on-one meetings, or present a digital portfolio to those who cannot attend in person.

With social media, you can extend the impact of an event before, during, and after the live sessions. Pre-event activity on Facebook, Twitter, LinkedIn, and blogs can poll prospective attendees, ask for questions in advance, and engage participants in conversations related to your theme or topics. During the event, have staff members upload photos and videos to social media, Tweet and write Facebook posts about the event, capture the testimonials of attendees, and get action clips of speakers. Afterward, keep the momentum going by engaging participants in forums related to keynote or breakout topics, and ask attendees to post their own photos, videos, and comments.

You can use many of these same techniques to expand a virtual event. Add online classrooms or forums through Moodle or Ning sites, and the event moves beyond a simple phone call or Webinar. Schedule multiple speakers on a single day or create a multi-session event with many presenters over a series of days, and now you have a virtual summit. Extend the life of the event by capturing audio, video, and handouts in an infoproduct which can be experienced by people who could not attend the sessions live. Or, use the virtual event to create an ongoing community by launching a mastermind or mentoring program based on the themes of the online conference.

You could also make the leap to a complete virtual trade show, complete with vendor area, meeting rooms, product demonstrations, and attendees using computer-generated avatars to move through event spaces and interact with others in real time. Virtual trade shows have the advantage of being location independent, and eliminate both the hassle and expense of travel for attendees. On the other hand, while the teleseminars and Webinars discussed thus far are easy for small businesses to create and manage themselves on a shoestring budget, the complexity of a virtual trade show requires the assistance of one of the many companies dedicated to creating these intricate events, at a substantially greater cost.

Getting the Word Out About Your Live or Virtual Event

Whether your event is live or virtual, you can make a tremendous productivity boost by using the growing number of event management and promotion tools available online. These cloud-based programs make it possible to register attendees; collect information about participants' opinions, interests, and contact data; handle and track payments; and produce reports.

Most programs also incorporate templates to send e-mail invitations to your opt-in list, promote your event on social media and via online event listings, stay in touch with participants, and recruit and manage affiliates to help publicize your event.

For a small event such as a reception, Evite.com enables users to create free invitations with online RSVP and tracking capability. Evite's library of templates gives you a wide range of options to choose from, ranging from informal to professional. You've even got the ability to poll your guests for preferences on things such as food, music, or activities, or to enable guests to sign up to bring something for the event. While Evite is great for small gatherings, it isn't designed to handle large events, paid registration, or more complex reporting.

Facebook offers the ability to create an event page especially for your upcoming live or virtual program. You can use the event page to invite your Facebook friends, the people who have "liked" your business page, and people who aren't even on Facebook. You can even limit your invitation to go to particular groups of friends if you have already set up friend lists within Facebook. Unfortunately, at the time of this writing, Facebook event pages could not support recurring events, so you will need to create a new page for each instance of an event.

LinkedIn also makes it possible to announce and promote events. You can list your own event, search events listed by others, and see which people in your professional network are planning to attend listed events. LinkedIn's event feature also gives you the ability to RSVP for an event invitation, and receive updates on events which you have indicated you plan to attend. LinkedIn also partners with Eventbrite, which is an online event management site, so LinkedIn event users also receive information about upcoming programs listed through Eventbrite.

Constant Contact is well-known for its e-mail marketing product, but it also has a multifaceted event promotion and management program. The Constant Contact program covers event registration, attendee RSVPs, secure online payment processing, tracking and reporting, and even a customized event homepage. If you are already using Constant Contact for your e-mail, the program makes it simple to send out e-mail invitations and push your event information out to social media. For those accustomed to Constant Contact's templates and functionality, the event marketing add-on is easy to use. You can even share your upcoming calendar of events via a link in blog posts, your e-mail signature, or other online articles.

If you're planning a recurring event, explore Meetup.com. Meetup allows you to create a group and announce recurring group meetings, along with dates, times, locations, and other details. Meetup also gives you a home page for the group and has embedded e-mail and online forum capabilities. Attendees can add comments and rate recent events.

Other sites that provide similar combinations of event marketing and management include Ettend.com, Eventish.com, Signupguy.com, and Eventsbot.com, to name just a few. Programs vary in the range of services included and in pricing, as well as ease of use. Some programs are free as long as the event does not charge admission. For paid events, pricing varies from a flat monthly fee to a per-ticket charge and/or a percentage of the ticket price. Do the math to make sure you find the program that provides the best range of services at a price you can afford.

If you'll be charging for tickets, decide up front how you'll handle sales. If you're already using an online shopping cart, you may want to run all ticket sales through that program. If you don't have a shopping cart program or if it isn't designed for handling event ticket sales, many of the event management programs have a built-in secure shopping cart. If you're planning to use affiliates to help promote your event to a broader audience, make sure your shopping cart can generate unique affiliate links and track affiliate sales. Think ahead about your need for things like coupon codes, complimentary passes, or paid sponsorships, and make sure your choice of online shopping cart can handle what you need.

For example, Ettend makes it easy to create a customized event Website and to add an event blog, and provides flexibility for handling different time zones and currencies. It can integrate with social media and has an internal e-mail marketing functionality, and uses both SEO and RSS to help spread the word about your event. It can also handle sponsors and promotional codes, a nice feature if you need it. Ettend also has a reminder feature to keep attendees in the loop, and has robust tracking and reporting features.

Eventish can handle events that sell tickets as well as banquet-style programs requiring table seating. It even has the ability to create floor plans and seating assignments. It can handle ticketing for multiple dates, and also provides a range of event promotion tools, including integration with social media.

Some sites charge a per-ticket fee plus a percentage of the transaction cost. Determine in advance whether you'll be building those charges into the ticket price or absorbing them. Then look for a program which gives you a choice in how to structure your pricing. SignUpGuy.com and some other sites make it possible for you to decide who pays the added costs. SignUpGuy also offers additional services such as stuffing and shipping promotional bags.

RegOnline.com offers the ability to add a social networking community to your event where attendees can connect online. It can also collect and group all the social media conversation about your event into one convenient portal, and create a directory of attendees (with opt-in) to make it easy for participants to find each other and network before and after the event. Another nice feature is its event distribution service, which can submit your event to online event directories. RegOnline can also create a mobile event app for the meeting organizer and help with badge creation and on-site registration.

Depending on the level of service you choose (free basic service or a more extended, paid premium service), Eventsbot offers some nice extras to its event management and promotion capabilities. It can create unique URLs for every event, integrated with the home Website of the organization presenting the event. It enables planners to copy or repeat events without having to start over again, and it can generate e-mail alerts to confirm registration automatically for both attendees and event organizers.

Whether you choose to organize your event online or as a live program, virtual event management and marketing programs can provide a big productivity boost for a minimal cost. If you've ever run a large event, you know that the devil is in the details and that an event planner can never have too much help or be too organized. These tools can provide both structure and the kind of processing, promotional, and tracking services that it would otherwise require a large staff to achieve. They're worth checking out, especially if you'd rather be making connections at your event instead of taking tickets.

Results Reminder

! Congestion, tight schedules, parking challenges, and high gas prices can make online events very attractive for both attendees and presenters.

Rule of 30

30

What are 30 key tasks that are essential to the success of your event? How can you automate them to increase your productivity and save both time and money?

Action Items

1. Check out these and other online event management and marketing services, and do the math to determine the pricing structure that would work best for your upcoming programs.

2. If you haven't considered doing all or part of your event virtually, maybe it's time to rethink your choice. If you're already hosting a virtual event, look for ways you could improve productivity, handle processing more effectively, or extend your reach and visibility.

27
Virtual Deals
and Coupons

Part of being productive is knowing how to make the most of your resources, especially when it comes to time and money. Getting more for your money helps you use your cash resources as efficiently as possible, and using time-saving ways to get the best deals heightens the productivity of both your time and your cash.

Realize that your customers also want to be more productive, and when you help them achieve their productivity goals, they'll reward you with their business. So while it's great when you get a good deal yourself, it's also good when you can provide a great deal for your customers. That's why it's important to know how virtual deals and coupons work—so you can get them and give them.

Give First, and Reap the Rewards

In order to be able to give your customers special deals and coupons, you need to work with an online shopping cart that supports different pricing tiers, coupon codes, and other discounts. I've already talked about the basic features of online shopping carts and how to choose a program that meets your needs. Be sure that you think beyond just collecting payments to how you might be able to offer attractive discounts on a seasonal or special offer basis.

Don't just think about discounts as being a way to get new customers. Offering a loyalty discount can win repeat or upsell business from your current customers. This can be as easy as providing a special coupon code—if your shopping cart can accept special codes.

Providing the code doesn't have to be difficult. Constant Contact includes a coupon in many of its newsletter templates. This is the perfect place to reward your opt-in followers with special offers. You can also thank the people who have "liked" your Facebook page, who follow you on Twitter, or who read your blog. Or, reward the people who find your business through sites like Groupon or Yelp, or the Foursquare participants who frequent your location. (Rewarding your social media followers encourages new people to join your newsletter or connect on social media in order to get the discounts.) Or, you can go beyond simple couponing with programs such as BuildACouponSite.com, ModularMerchant.com, or CouponFusion.com. Before signing up for an extra program, make sure you fully understand the capabilities of your existing shopping cart; you may already have the capability that you need.

If you have the type of business that works well with loyalty cards, consider creating a mobile phone app that assures your best customers will always get the benefit of their reward card. Developing custom apps is getting easier and less expensive as more and more people embrace the use of smartphones. You can use a site such as Mobile.Conduit.com, Saasmob.com, or other programs to create your own app, or use one of the many companies that will create apps for you.

Giving Is Nice, But So Is Getting

As beneficial as it can be to provide online discounts and rewards to your customers, it's pretty nice to land some good deals yourself. Mobile technology is making it easier than ever to assure that you can access your coupons, reward points, and discounts wherever you carry your phone. Apps also help you make more productive use of your time by helping you search for and find the products you want, and to compare availability and pricing.

AAA (American Automobile Association) has long been known for the special discounts it arranges for members with all kinds of dining, hospitality, and travel-related companies. Now, there's an app for AAA that will use your current location to alert you to nearby merchants that offer AAA discounts. The app will even provide detailed directions to help you reach the merchant you select.

For those who are true believers in the value of coupons but hate to clip and carry all that paper, consider some of the coupon apps available for smartphones and tablet PCs. Coupon Sherpa, AFullCup, Shopper, and MobileCoupons all help you find, organize, and store digital coupons so that you've got what you need wherever you go.

Groupon, Living Social, Daily Shopper, and MobiQpons also provide online discounts and coupons. Most permit you to search by location, store, and product type. Other sites, such as Foursquare, reward frequent customers with special discounts. Getyowza.com and The Coupons App are more options. Try out several of these apps; you're likely to find that some apps are more in tune with your shopping habits and tastes than others.

You can save a lot of money by comparison shopping, but who has time? You do—with the right apps. Loading Amazon's app not only makes it easy to buy from this online retail giant, it also makes it simple to check prices to see if Amazon has a better deal. Not sure what size product to purchase to get the most for your money? CompareMe is an app that makes it easy to decide which package gets you the best price.

QR (Quick Response) codes are popping up everywhere. Many QR codes lead straight to discounts and deals, so make sure you have a QR code reader on your phone. Annoyed that merchants often don't put a price sticker on individual items? You'll always know what something costs when you've got the Barcode Reader app on your phone. Not only does Barcode Reader scan the code and tell you the price, but it will helpfully fetch prices for that item from other retailers so you can get the best deal.

If you travel, make sure that you check your frequent flyer, credit card rewards program, hotel loyalty program, and favorite car rental companies to see if they have apps and offer special online discounts. Hertz Car Rental not only has an app to help you make reservations, but it offers special weekly deals just for smartphone users. Hotel Tonight is an app that provides daily specials and helps you find low prices on hotel rooms wherever you travel. Omni Hotels has an app that not only makes it easy to find and book an Omni room, but it also provides special offers for app users. Priceline has an app for finding hotel and car rental discounts. Star Alliance (the consortium of airlines that includes USAirways, Air Canada, Continental, Lufthansa, and United, among others) has a FareFinder app that will search for flights to your chosen destination across all of its member airlines to help you find the best flights and pricing.

Expect more and more membership organizations, professional/ business associations, and other groups to begin offering their discounts to members via apps. You've paid your dues, so make sure you get everything included in your membership.

Results Reminder

!

Apps that help you save time are also helping you save money, and give you more productive time in your day.

Rule of 30

30

What are the 30 products or services you buy most frequently? Which merchants do you prefer? If they don't already have dedicated apps, they probably will soon.

Action Items

1. Think about your daily, weekly, and monthly buying habits, then go online to find apps to help you use these products/services more efficiently or qualify for special discounts.

2. Think about how your ideal customers buy from you. How could you reward them and increase repeat purchases by creating online deals, downloadable coupons, or even a customized app?

28
Free (and Almost Free) PR and Marketing

In your quest to expand your contacts and grow your business, it's essential to remain consistently visible. Personal networking (live and virtual) is part of that equation, but PR and marketing also play an important role to help you broaden your reach.

Public relations (PR) is all about getting unpaid publicity by seeding the media with press releases, article pitches, and story ideas so that you and your business get mentioned without paying for the exposure. Marketing, on the other hand, usually involves some expense, although there are ways to keep costs very low and still be effective. Your see productivity gains when your PR and marketing efforts reap rewards for a minimum investment of time and money.

The PR Advantage

In the pre-Internet days, PR was all about targeting your news to reach the newspaper/magazine editors, journalists, and radio/TV hosts who controlled what information reached the reading or listening public. Press releases, story ideas, and article pitches had a finite potential audience, since there were only so many magazines, newspapers, radio stations, and TV stations available. In the old days, those journalists and gatekeepers were your first audience, because if you couldn't sell them on your story, it would never reach the public.

Today's PR world is very different, thanks to the Internet. Many print publications have either ceased production or moved to an online-only format. The remaining print publications have created Websites where they post extended news coverage. At the same time, as newspapers and magazines have struggled to reinvent themselves and survive, most editorial staffs have cut in-house reporting on life-style issues, books, travel, product and food reviews, and other "soft" news.

Coverage of those issues didn't go away; a host of citizen-journalists rushed in to fill the gap with blogs, Websites, and social media pages dedicated to topics no longer covered in the "official" media. At the same time, advances in technology created the ability for anyone to easily load Web audio and video. YouTube and similar video channels sprang up, creating on-demand programming that allowed users to select and share content they wanted to see when they wanted to see it. Internet radio (streaming audio, really, since no FCC licensing or airwave broadcasting is involved) made it possible for hosts with a passion for a specialized topic to find a responsive niche audience anywhere in the world.

Instead of seeing media opportunities contract, these new online formats have created an explosion of opportunities for small-business owners and experts to be heard and remain visible. (I go more deeply into the nitty-gritty of creating and pitching press releases in my book 30 Days to Online PR and Marketing Success.) You now have an almost unlimited opportunity to tell your story online and reach a global audience—for free. And remember this: any content you post to the Web becomes searchable, which improves your search engine results, boosting your SEO.

The heart of online PR lies in posting your press releases to online distribution sites where reporters and bloggers can find them and pick them up. Some of these sites allow you to post your releases for free, while others charge fees that vary from very little to several hundred dollars.

What's the difference between the paid sites and the free sites? In a nutshell: organization and distribution. On the free sites, your release will be listed on the site's home page, but won't be sent out to specialized lists of reporters at regional or national publications. You'll benefit from online visibility and searchability, but these sites won't put you on the Associated Press wire. That's okay. Now that press releases can be posted on the Internet, consumers can gather their information directly, without needing to read about your product/service in a magazine or blog. This is a valuable information stream, so it's worth it to post on the free sites. Some of the best free sites out there include 1888PressRelease.com, 24-7PressRelease. com, OpenPR.com, and PRLog.com, but there are also many others.

So why pay for PR postings? Again, the answer lies in organization and distribution. The paid sites enable you to target your release to clusters of online, regional, and national publications by industry or topic. Some of these sites have been in the business of press release distribution since before the Internet, and they have a longtime reputation with journalists as being a trusted source for news. Because it costs money to post releases on the bigger sites, there are fewer "junk" releases of dubious value. Also, the bigger sites usually offer a level of distribution that includes the AP and United Press International (UPI) news feeds, increasing your distribution to well-known publications. Some of the best-known paid sites include PRWeb.com, PRLeap.com, and PRNewswire.com.

Internet radio and podcasting (creating downloadable audio) have also broadened your interview opportunities. Shows exist for nearly every topic, hobby, business, and interest, unfettered by the need to sell advertising to cover the costs traditional radio had to sustain (licenses, studios, full-time staff, and so on). BlogTalkRadio.com, PodcastAlley.com, DivaToolBox.com, and PodcastPickle.com are just some of the places you can search for shows that would be a good fit for your expertise.

Some bloggers scan press release sites for ideas, but many don't. Yet you can reach hundreds to tens of thousands of people by being interviewed or featured in a blog dedicated to your topic or industry. Start your quest to be a guest blogger by checking out sites such as MyBlogGuest.com, which helps bloggers seeking guests to match up with guests seeking blog exposure. Or, compile your own list of blogs that cover your topic and build relationships with the bloggers, leading up to requesting that they allow you to provide guest blog posts or feature your topic. (I cover this in a lot more detail in 30 *Days to Online PR and Marketing Success*, but I want to plant the seed here, because the ability to spread the word online is a huge productivity booster.)

Online Marketing Takes Off

While free PR can get you mentioned in major publications, you don't get to control when or where that placement occurs, or even assure that it will happen. With paid marketing, you choose where your ads run, how often they are seen, and how much you invest. While paid advertising in print and traditional radio have always been available, the Internet has created fantastic new opportunities, many of which are available at a fraction of the cost.

Social media is an effective form of online marketing that is absolutely free. Actually, social media is really good old-fashioned networking on a new platform. It's really more about creating relationships and extending your network than it is hard sales, and people who succeed in using social media grasp that difference. Getting people to "like" your Facebook business page, or become your Facebook friend or your Twitter follower, is really another way of adding to your opt-in list. (Constant Contact users can go to the Constant Contact Labs section on Facebook to grab the code for a "join my mailing list" box that works with Facebook, blogs, and Websites to funnel online friends into your permission-based e-mail newsletter list as well.)

Facebook and LinkedIn also offer paid advertising. Facebook ads are extremely easy to create and allow you the ability to pick the demographics of the audience you want to see the ad. You can set your lifetime and daily budgets, and make many more choices to customize the ads to your needs. Using Facebook ads, you can reach millions of people for just a few hundred dollars.

LinkedIn ads work in much the same way. You choose the graphic and write the short ad copy. You set the budget, and you pay for impressions or clicks. As with Facebook ads, you get to determine the characteristics of the people who will see your ad.

Both Facebook and LinkedIn ads are strengthened by the power of community. Ads are placed by community members for community members, much like a local newspaper. Ads can introduce you to people who haven't heard of your services before and encourage people who know you by reputation to learn more. Facebook and LinkedIn ads enable viewers to click through the ad to a destination page—most often, either to your profile or to your Website. This can be a great way to build traffic and to encourage people you know in one community to connect with you on another platform, explore your Website, or be exposed to your opt-in incentive.

A growing number of blogs, podcasts, and Internet radio shows also accept advertising. If you find a site that is a perfect fit and has a large audience of your ideal clients, you may want to experiment with placing an ad. As with the Facebook and LinkedIn ads, the goal is not only visibility, but also enabling people to link through the ad to another destination page where they can make a permission-based connection with you.

Even in today's online world, the need remains for some printed marketing materials, such as business cards, banners, bookmarks, and promotional items. Vistaprint.com and GotPrint.com are two sites that offer extremely low pricing with very good quality. Be sure to include QR codes on all your printed materials to make it easy for smartphone users to click through to your Website or social media pages.

I've just scratched the surface on online PR and marketing, but it's important to include these essential functions, since they make a huge impact on your ability to extend your network and grow your business. By learning to use apps, cloud-based programs, and online services, you can increase your productivity while significantly decreasing your costs. If you want to learn more on this subject, please take a look at my other books, *30 Days to Social Media Success* and *30 Days to Online PR and Marketing Success*.

Results Reminder

! Prospects buy when their need is urgent, not necessarily when they receive information about your company. Online PR and marketing help you remain visible until prospects are ready to buy.

Rule of 30

30

It takes seven to 30 "touches" to turn a window shopper into a buyer. PR placements and online marketing can help you vary your touches for more success.

Action Items

1. Spend some time on Facebook and LinkedIn and pay particular attention to the ads others have placed. What do you like? What turns you off? Which ads make you want to click through?

2. Think about the number of newsworthy activities your company has in a year: special events, significant hires, new products or locations, awards or honors, community service participation, etc. These are all opportunities for PR exposure. For best results, space out newsworthy events throughout the year so that you remain consistently visible.

29
Promoting With Web Audio, Video, and Photos

If it's true that a picture is worth a thousand words, then adding visuals to your communication efforts is in itself a huge productivity boost. Human beings respond to images, movement, and sound. One way to make your efforts to grow your business and extend your network more productive and effective is to incorporate sight, sound, and motion into your online presence.

The Magic Of Your Voice

We make a lot of judgments about people from non-verbal cues; in fact, scientists tell us that the vast majority of our first impressions of people we meet are made from their facial expression, tone of voice, posture, and other indicators that have nothing to do with the words they actually speak.

From birth onward, sound is one of our most crucial cues to read the world around us. Our interpersonal relationships also hinge on our ability to correctly interpret the tone of voice used to address us. First as children and then throughout life, we find comfort in soothing voices. Tone of voice also conveys authority, friendliness, knowledge, and inclusiveness. With all that going for it, why not add your voice to your Website, social media, e-newsletter, and other online resources, especially when Web audio is simple and easy?

Start with a program such as AudioAcrobat or InstantTeleseminar. These programs make it very easy to record your voice using a regular phone call. You can record a greeting for your Webpage, a holiday message for your newsletter, a short tip for your social media pages, or a reading from something you've recently written; it's up to you.

AudioAcrobat enables you to share your audio in several different formats. If you want to provide audio with a three-button player bar, AudioAcrobat (and similar programs) will provide you the HTML code to drop into your site. Or, if you'd prefer to just share a link that will play when clicked (best for newsletters), the program will generate that, too. Have an audience that prefers to download and listen later? You can also easily create a download link for your audio so that your audience can save your audio and play it whenever it's convenient.

Audio can make your online sites more welcoming, because it helps to provide more clues about you and your personality. As your audience comes to recognize your voice, they begin to feel like they know you personally. If you're staying in touch with people who have met you in person, your voice should be both familiar and a reminder of a pleasant prior meeting.

You can take Web audio further and extend your contacts by creating podcasts or Internet radio shows. A podcast is a recorded audio series that can be streamed via the Internet or downloaded onto a disk or MP3 player. Podcasts exist for just about every industry, area of expertise, hobby, or interest. Some podcasts are as short as five minutes long (such as the wildly popular GrammarGirl (http://grammar.quickanddirtytips.com/) or as long as an hour or more. How long you make your podcast depends on your audience's attention span, the amount of time you can commit on a regular basis, and the type of information you want to share.

For example, if you sell gourmet kitchen notions, you might create a podcast about cooking with local, fresh, seasonal herbs. Or, if you're a dog trainer, create a podcast on overcoming common pet misbehavior. Podcasts range from offering new episodes daily to providing something every week or just a couple of times a month. The important thing is to pick a schedule and stick to it. You can also archive your past episodes so people can find the ones they missed. AudioAcrobat makes it easy to upload your podcasts to iTunes so you can share them with the world.

"Internet radio" really refers to Web audio programs broadcast online and often grouped together on sites such as BlogTalkRadio or DivaToolBox. Internet radio shows usually air live and are then recorded and provided later as podcasts. Some Internet radio shows have very small audiences, but others number their audiences and downloads in the tens of thousands or even millions. It's a commitment to create a live regular show, but it also positions you to reach out to noted experts in your industry and other people who can become valuable professional contacts. And it provides ongoing expert visibility for you and your company. Some shows gather a large enough audience that they create revenue through online ad sales and sponsorships. Most shows are produced as a labor of love or as a marketing outreach, where the reward is the show itself and the connections and visibility it creates.

Sight and Motion Make an Impact

Web video and photos can do a lot to make visitors to your online sites feel as if they've met you. Video clips of your speaking engagements, photos from business events, carefully selected personal/casual pictures, and short video tips can all bring your e-mail newsletters, blogs, home pages, and social media sites to life. When visitors get a chance to see you in action, it increases their comfort level with you because you are no longer a stranger. Hearing and seeing you can reinforce your professional credibility with people who haven't had the chance to meet you in person. And you may be surprised to find that creating your own videos can be fun.

Recording Web video is easy. Many new laptops have a video recording feature built in, and may also include simple video editing software (if not, it's inexpensive for your basic needs). Or, you can use the video capability on your smartphone or digital camera for short clips. For a longer video (for example, a speaking presentation), you can use a digital video camera.

Short clips are easy to upload to YouTube, which makes sharing simple. Upload your video (keep it under nine minutes—one to three minutes is best) and fill out the keywords to make it searchable. Be sure you include a compelling description so people will know the benefit of watching it, and make sure to include your Web address near the beginning of your description, so people who just scan the description can find you online. For best results, create videos on a regular schedule, such as once a week or at least once a month to keep people interested. YouTube also gives you the ability to create your own "channel," so that people who like your videos can subscribe and never miss a new post.

You can also upload your videos to AudioAcrobat, which formats them for easy sharing: as a play-now link, as a download link, or in the three-button format. Through AudioAcrobat, you can also share your videos to iTunes or add them to your podcast as bonus material.

TalkFusion is another way to share your Web video in an e-mail newsletter format designed to optimize shared video. TalkFusion makes it easy to create video blogs, video autoresponders, and even live video broadcasting and conferencing. It also provides templates to help you deliver and showcase your videos to your best advantage.

With all the buzz about video, don't overlook the power of still photos. Everyone enjoys browsing through someone else's photos, and you can share photos to increase your connectedness to your audience. For best results, share an assortment of professional and "business casual" photos. Professional photos might include pictures of you taken at conferences, trade shows, and seminars that you attend or where you are a speaker. Or, ask your customers to send you photos to post showing them using your product. Take photos of your staff at work, of you at your trade show booth, or of you with clients. (Get permission before uploading photos of other people.)

"Business casual" photos are ones that provide a glimpse of your life beyond work. Think of the kinds of topics you discuss when you make small talk at a networking program: sporting events you've attended, recent vacations, hobbies, family milestones. It's fine to toss in some of these types of photos, because it humanizes you and helps people feel as if they're getting to know the person behind the business. Obviously, you only want to post photos that will enhance, and not sabotage, your professional reputation, so avoid pictures in which everyone is holding a cocktail or looking disheveled. Whether or not you post pictures of family (children, spouse, pets) is a personal decision, and depends on your particular comfort level and concept of privacy and security. I'm more okay with posting photos of adult children than of small children, just for safety's sake. But you may find tremendous response from your audience on pictures of a new grandchild, photos from a recent family wedding, and so on. You'll have to make that call for yourself.

Flickr is a well-known photo sharing site, but be aware it does not like overtly commercial photos, such as logos and product shots. Picasa is a Google site, so it can make integrating with your other Google accounts very easy. Photobucket is another popular site, as is Facebook. Always be sure to read and abide by the terms of service so your photos don't get you bounced from the system. Be sure to tag your photos so that they're searchable (which gives you an SEO boost), and so that they help increase visibility for you and your business. Many photo and video sharing sites have grown into offering social media–style sharing, online forums, and other features.

Photos are a powerful way to connect. You never know when a photo you've shared online may spark a conversation with a client or prospect that leads to new business!

Results Reminder

!

A picture is truly worth a thousand words. What photos could you post to help your online readers feel they've met you?

Rule of 30

30

When you're out and about for business, snap a few photos, then spend 30 minutes a month tagging and sharing.

Action Items

1. How can you tap into the power of Web audio for your business? What tips or information could you share in short audios (or longer podcasts or downloadable classes) that could deepen your relationship with your online audience?

2. Video gives the impression that you've seen someone in action. Where would it be most powerful for your online audience to see you in action? How can you create short Web video to enhance your Web visitors' experience?

30
Viral Marketing: Getting Your Customers to Promote for You

Wouldn't it be nice if you could get your customers to promote your company for you—for free? That's what happens with viral marketing. Viral marketing is like old-fashioned word of mouth on steroids. In the old days, word of mouth was limited to the people your customers saw, wrote to, or called on the phone. With the Internet, word of mouth can go around the globe at the speed of light, reaching thousands or millions of people within seconds of the final keystroke. It's the ultimate in productivity, since others are doing the marketing on your behalf, and it also can have a huge impact on expanding your contacts and helping you grow your business.

Opinions aren't the only thing that can go viral; content that intrigues or entertains readers/viewers can also suddenly receive millions of hits when users pass it along to their friends. Sometimes this happens by accident, but there are ways you can help your content receive more notice, which just might nudge it into viral status.

Make It Easy to Share

Help your content go viral by making it easy to share. Constant Contact gives you the option to add a "share bar" to your newsletters, so your recipients can easily share the content on their Facebook, Twitter, and other social networks. You may want to educate your readers about what the share bar is and how to use it, and include a personal request for them to pass it along via social media. Constant Contact also gives you a one-click ability to share your newsletter to your own Facebook, Twitter, and other sites. Add a line or two to create interest in the link so your friends and followers will have a reason to click through.

You can create the same type of share bar on your other sites with AddThis. AddThis generates a share bar and gives you the HTML code to add to your blog, Website, and other pages to make it easy for readers to pass along content they find interesting. ShareThis and Lockerz Share (http://share.lockerz.com/) are other similar services.

Earlier in the book, I talked about social bookmarking sites such as Digg, Delicious, and StumbleUpon. These are great sites to help get your content noticed (and hopefully shared) by a large readership. YouTube and other photo/video sites also make it easy to share by including a link you can pass along via e-mail or page posts.

The "like" button on Facebook is another way of sharing content, because when one of your readers says they "like" a post, a notification automatically goes to all of their Facebook fans or friends, alerting them and sharing a link.

How do you get readers to share? It's really a two-fold process. First, educate your readers about why they want to share content. Some readers, especially those who are fairly new to using social media, may not really understand how to share, so you can explain how it works. Let them know what's in it for them when they share: they provide interesting, humorous or informative content to their readers without having to create that content themselves, and they enhance their reputation of being the person with the news. Then, let them know you would appreciate them sharing your content and helping you reach more people.

The second part of the process lies in creating content interesting enough for people to want to share it. Take a hard look at the majority of your posts. Are they helpful, funny, provocative, unusual, or intriguing? Does your voice, personality, or sense of humor come through in a way that makes even mundane information sparkle? Do you share a unique perspective or have a different way of coming at a topic? These are all reasons people would want to share your content.

Make Sharing a Game

People like to have fun, even those who go online primarily for business. That's one reason why humorous content is shared so often; it provides a few moments' distraction from more serious concerns. So in addition to making sharing easy, why not make it fun?

Because people like to see information about themselves, many online promotions have invited customers to upload photos of themselves using the product, carrying their product to exotic locations, or doing something seasonal with their product. Kodak, for example, has invited people to upload photos of their pets in Christmas costumes. Heinz ketchup invited ketchup lovers to upload videos telling the world about their favorite ways to eat ketchup. Summit Coffee, a local North Carolina coffee shop, invites its customers to photograph themselves holding a Summit logo in exotic and remote vacation spots. Often, just being able to have bragging rights about being posted on a famous company's Website is reward enough. Just think: every person whose photo is posted during one of these promotions is likely to share the link with hundreds of their online friends, driving traffic and visibility for the company hosting the promotion—and it's all free.

Creating this type of promotion is simple and fun. You'll have to create the landing page on your blog, social media pages, and Website, and assure that photos or videos get posted quickly. Make sure that everyone sending an entry completes a simple release form giving you permission to add their content, and while you're at it, capture their contact information so you have permission to stay in touch. And you'll need to publicize the promotion through PR and your own content, perhaps even adding some online marketing. But think about the potential return as participants pass along links to their friends to show them where you've posted their photos or video. To take full advantage of the traffic, make sure you have a clear offer of a free trial, no-cost download, or other incentive to encourage newcomers to opt in to your mailing list. Celebrate the promotion's success by sending out a release at the end mentioning how many entries were posted. You might even want to send a thank-you e-mail with a link to free bonus downloadable content (or a coupon or tip sheet) to all those who opted in. Or, do random drawings with small downloadable prizes or discount coupons, picking from those who post content and comment on the postings to keep interest high.

As with anything that might appear to be a contest, avoid requiring a purchase to participate, and check the laws in your area, as they vary by state or province.

Facebook has tightened its rules regarding contests. Before doing anything contest-oriented on Facebook, make sure you check the site's rules so your page doesn't get shut down. Or, create your contest through a service such as PinpointSocial or Constant Contact, which provide Facebook-compliant, template-driven contests that make it easy for users to create and post their own social media contests. You can create promotions to offer free downloadable content (such as an article) to encourage people to "like" your page and increase traffic. You also receive reports to let you know just how well your contest is doing.

Another way to go viral is to create a really useful mobile app related to your business. First, decide what kind of app might appeal to prospects and customers. For some companies, such as those in the news or entertainment business, an app that streams recent posts to the company blog or social media site (things such as dinner specials or live music, for example), might be as sophisticated as you need to get. If that's all you need, you might even try creating the app with a do-it-yourself service such as App.co (http://app.co/).

The next easiest way to create an app is to brand a utilitarian app that is related to the product you serve. This is the mobile app equivalent of handing out imprinted advertising specialty items, such as calculators, pens, or mugs with your logo on them. Except in this case, your logo and branding are on a mobile app instead of a tangible item.

Do you help people lose weight? Why not offer a branded calorie counter app to help them track their eating habits, or an app that lets people calculate calories in popular grocery items? Yes, these types of apps already exist, but not yet with your logo on them. Are you hosting an event? How about providing an app that provides the updated schedule and enables users to create their own customized agenda of presentations they want to attend. These are just a few examples of what is possible with branded apps. Or, create an app that makes it easy to place an online order, request items for takeout, or schedule an appointment. The important thing is that your app be seen as useful and possibly even fun by your target audience. Create a particularly useful app, and it just might go viral—with your branding all over it.

As of the time of this writing, there aren't a lot of template-driven app creation sites—yet. As mobile apps grow as a marketing and branding tool, I think we'll see template programs to make it easier and less expensive for people to create branded apps. For now, you'll need to work with an app design firm. Don't let that scare you. Branding a common utility app (such as a calculator, flashlight, or note pad) is less involved than creating a game app or other customized content. Just make sure you understand what is involved to keep the app running smoothly so users remain satisfied.

The secret to creating viral content is to know what appeals to your customer base and then giving it to them, and if possible, creating some fun or excitement in the process. You've really become productive when your customers are excited about doing your marketing for you!

Results Reminder

! Inject humor and personality into your highly useful content to increase your chance of going viral.

Rule of 30

30

What are 30 possible ways you could involve your online audience in a photo or video contest related to your product or service?

Action Items

1. Spend some time surfing the Web for examples of online contests that might be adaptable for your business.

2. Browse iTunes' App Store and other app sites to see how companies are branding mobile apps. Do you get any ideas for an app you could create for your business?

Afterword: Where Do I Go From Here?

Now that you've gotten many ideas on how to improve your virtual productivity, expand your contacts and grow your business, how do you make it happen?

Productivity increases require behavior changes. For example, it may take you a few months to completely wean yourself from using a paper appointment book and moving to an online scheduler. That's okay. Give yourself permission to need some time to change your habits and get comfortable with the technology. Just don't put off making the change because of the temporary discomfort involved in trying something new.

Real productivity happens when techniques are applied over time. At first, you may feel less productive as you get used to using new technology or change the way you're used to doing something. But when you stick with it, you'll see productivity improve, and your learning curve will pay off.

Technology changes rapidly. By the time you read this book, there are likely to be new sites, apps, programs, and services that weren't available when the book was written. Make it a habit to keep your eyes open for new offerings that build on the principles I've shared in this book, and incorporate them into your routine to see continued productivity enhancement.

When it comes to expanding your contacts, remember that the Internet is a large community with dedicated smaller communities. When you begin making connections through a new social media or online membership site, go slowly, and keep your primary focus on being a good community member. Be helpful, add value, and always be polite and professional, and you will begin to create those new connections that can increase your influence in amazing ways.

Much of the same is true when it comes to online efforts to grow your business. The techniques I've shared in this book are proven, but not necessarily immediate. As with the effort necessary to establish yourself as a trusted member of any community, reaping online sales from your social media, online PR, and Internet marketing strategies doesn't always happen overnight. Not only does it take time to spread the word, but it also takes time to earn the trust of prospective customers. Purchasers buy when the need is urgent for them, not just because you've posted a campaign or a press release. Yet everything you do online, every way in which you increase the consistent visibility of your brand, helps to assure that when prospects do reach the time to make a purchase, your company, product, or service will be top of mind. That is a huge advantage, and something that directly factors into the likelihood that prospects will decide to buy from you.

In other words, although the Internet can serve up search results in a matter of seconds, it can't guarantee that results from your online networking, productivity, and promotional efforts will be equally instantaneous. Patience is required to see real results, and this is where many business owners go off track. Always remember that on the other side of the computer is a human being, a real person with his or her own needs, fears, and busy schedule. Computers react immediately, but people don't. They need to be educated, wooed, reasoned with, and given incentives. They may gather information for a while before taking action, and during that dormant phase, you won't be able to fully appreciate the impact your online efforts are having. Be patient. Results happen when you work your strategy with a clear goal in mind and communicate a clear message to your targeted audience.

As you explore what the Internet has to offer to help you improve your productivity, expand your contacts, and grow your business, remember that all three goals require you to be open to new ideas and adaptable to changing circumstances. Unexpected opportunities arise every day, and to gain the best results, you need to be looking for them and ready to take advantage of what they offer. So work your plan (it will definitely help you be more productive), but leave room for serendipity. The connection you make with a new person online might lead you to discover something unexpected that will help you further improve both productivity and business growth. Realizing high growth will require you to seek out even more ways to boost your productivity, and will simultaneously expand your network of contacts. Becoming more productive will free you up to spend more time growing your network and promoting your business. Productivity, promotion, and your personal network are all intertwined, and you'll see the biggest gains when you develop all three in sync with each other.

Finally, let go of your fears about the online world and be willing to explore with a sense of wonder and excitement. Be open to meeting people who may seem very different from you but who share your passion for a subject, or who have valuable knowledge to impart. Don't be afraid to try new things, whether they're mobile apps or Websites. Take reasonable precautions to protect your data and your computer system, but don't let your fears keep you from reaping the benefits of all the good things that the Internet has to offer. The same common sense and street smarts that enable you to safely navigate a big city will also help you explore the Internet. And as you do, you'll find that what you learn and the new resources you gain will change you and your business, even as what you offer changes your prospects and the Internet itself. Enjoy the journey.

Websites and Apps

1888pressrelease.com

1shoppingcart.com

24-7pressrelease.com

AddThis.com

AFullCup.com

Alexa.com

Amazon.com

Amazon WebPay: www.payments.amazon.com/sdui/sdui/personal/ money

Ambiance: http://itunes.apple.com/us/app/ambiance/ id285538312?mt=8

anyplace-control.com

App.co

Apple.com/icloud

Appzilla: http://itunes.apple.com/us/app/90-in-1-appzilla!/ id357716855?mt=8

186 30 Days to Virtual Productivity Success

Appzilla2: http://itunes.apple.com/us/app/appzilla-2-free!/id432012651?mt=8

AroundMe: http://itunes.apple.com/us/app/aroundme/id290051590?mt=

AudioAcrobat.com

Authorize.net

Awesome Note: http://itunes.apple.com/us/app/awesome-note-+to-do-diary/id320203391?mt=8

Barcode Reader: http://itunes.apple.com/us/app/barcode-reader/id340825499?mt=8

basecamphq.com

BaseOnline.com

Bento: http://itunes.apple.com/us/app/bento/id314638461?mt=8

Bitly.com

BizSnap: http://itunes.apple.com/us/app/bizsnap/id351056466?mt=8

BlogTalkRadio.com

Box.com

Box.net: http://itunes.apple.com/us/app/box-for-iphone-and-ipad/id290853822?mt=8

Bufferapp.com

BuildACouponSite.com

BusinessCardReader: http://itunes.apple.com/us/app/business-card-reader/id328175747?mt=8

businesscatalyst.com (Adobe)

CamScanner: http://itunes.apple.com/us/app/camscanner-free/id388627783?mt=8 or https://market.android.com/details?id=com.intsig.camscanner&hl=en

Carbonite.com

CardStar: http://itunes.apple.com/us/app/cardstar/id301460311?mt=8 or https://market.android.com/details?id=com.cardstar.android&hl=en

City Walks: http://itunes.apple.com/us/app/free-city-maps-walks-470+/id417207307?mt=8

CitySearch.com

ClockedIn.com

CompareMe: http://itunes.apple.com/us/app/compareme-shopping-utility/id300814524?mt=8

ConstantContact.com

ConsumerReports.org

Convertbot: http://itunes.apple.com/us/app/id308928075?mt=8

coopapp.com

CouponSherpa.com: http://itunes.apple.com/us/app/coupon-sherpa-mobile-coupons/id309938343?mt=8 or https://market.android.com/details?id=com.kinoli.couponsherpa&hl=en

Daily Shopper: http://itunes.apple.com/us/app/daily-shopper/id421594973?mt=8

Delicious.com

DeliveryStatus: http://itunes.apple.com/us/app/delivery-status-touch-package/id290986013?mt=8

Dictionary.com

Dictionary!: http://itunes.apple.com/us/app/dictionary!/id293283136?mt=8

Digg.com: http://itunes.apple.com/us/app/digg/id362872995?mt=8

DivaToolbox.com

Documents To Go Premium Office Suite: http://itunes.apple.com/us/app/documents-to-go-premium-office/id317107309?mt=8

Doodle.com

DragonDictation: www.nuance.com; http://itunes.apple.com/us/app/dragon-dictation/id341446764?mt=8

Dropbox.com: http://itunes.apple.com/us/app/dropbox/id327630330?mt=8 or https://market.android.com/details?id=com.dropbox.android&hl=en

EasyTimeSheet.com: http://itunes.apple.com/us/app/easy-timesheet-lite/id295601319?mt=8

Ebay.com: http://itunes.apple.com/us/app/ebay-for-ipad/id364203371?mt=8

Elance.com: https://www.google.com/enterprise/marketplace/viewListing?productListingId=6445+9442017978424625048

ElephantDrive.com

Ettend.com

Eventbrite.com: http://itunes.apple.com/us/app/entry-manager/id368260521?mt=8

Eventish.com: http://itunes.apple.com/us/app/eventish/id452259882?mt=8

Eventsbot.com

Evernote.com: http://itunes.apple.com/us/app/evernote/id281796108?mt=8 or https://market.android.com/details?id=com.evernote&hl=en

EveryTrail.com: http://itunes.apple.com/us/app/everytrail/id342467041?mt=8 or https://market.android.com/details?id=com.globalmotion.everytrail&hl=en

Evite.com: http://itunes.apple.com/us/app/evite/id431685286?mt=8

Facebook.com: http://itunes.apple.com/us/app/facebook/id284882215?mt=8 or https://market.android.com/details?id=com.facebook.katana&hl=en

Star Alliance FareFinder: http://itunes.apple.com/us/app/star-alliance-farefinder/id457852371?mt=8 or https://market.android.com/details?id=com.staralliance.android.farefinder&hl=en

FedEx Mobile: http://itunes.apple.com/us/app/fedex-mobile/id304462049?mt=8 or https://market.android.com/details?id=com.fedex.ida.android&hl=en

FilesToGo.com

Flickr.com: http://itunes.apple.com/us/app/flickr/id328407587?mt=8 or https://market.android.com/details?id=com.yahoo.mobile.client.android.flickr&hl=en

FlightAware.com: http://itunes.apple.com/us/app/flightaware-flight-tracker/id316793974?mt=8 or https://market.android.com/details?id=com.flightaware.android.liveFlightTracker&hl=en

FlightBoard: http://itunes.apple.com/us/app/id390553006?mt=8 or https://market.android.com/details?id=com.mobiata.flightboard&hl=en

FlightTrack: http://itunes.apple.com/us/app/id296240199?mt=8 or https://market.android.com/details?id=com.mobiata.flighttrack&hl=en

FolderShare (Windows Live Mesh): http://explore.live.com/windows-live-essentials-other-programs?T1=t4

foursquare.com; http://itunes.apple.com/us/app/foursquare/id306934924?mt=8 or https://market.android.com/details?id=com.joelapenna.foursquared&hl=en

FreeConference.com

FreeConferenceCall.com

Freelancer.com

FreeSaurus: http://itunes.apple.com/us/app/freesaurus-free-thesaurus!/
id299185772?mt=8

FreeTranslator: http://itunes.apple.com/us/app/free-translator/
id293855167?mt=8

Freshbooks.com: http://www.google.com/enterprise/marketplace/viewListing?
productListingId=3480+1736946957721454838

FriendFeed.com

FuzeMeeting.com: http://itunes.apple.com/us/app/fuze-meeting-hd/
id389446884?mt=8 or https://market.android.com/details?id=com.fuzebox.
fuze.android&hl=en

GasBuddy.com; http://itunes.apple.com/us/app/gasbuddy-find-cheap-gas-prices/
id406719683?mt=8 or https://market.android.com/developer?pub=GasBuddy.
com

Getyowza.com

Gist.com: http://itunes.apple.com/us/app/gist/id331790065?mt=8

GoDaddy.com: http://itunes.apple.com/us/app/godaddy.com-mobile-domain/
id333201813?mt=8 or https://market.android.com/details?id=com.godaddy.
mobile.android&hl=en

GoodReader: http://itunes.apple.com/us/app/goodreader-for-iphone/
id306277111?mt=8

Google.com: http://itunes.apple.com/us/app/google-search/
id284815942?mt=8 or https://market.android.com/details?id=com.google.
android.googlequicksearchbox&feature=more_from_developer#?t=W251bGws
MSwxLDEwMiwiY29tLmdvb2dsZS5hbmRyb2lkLmdvb2dsZXF1aWNrc2VhcmN
oYm94Il0.

Google.com/Calendar: http://itunes.apple.com/us/app/
calendars-google-calendar/id371434886?mt=8

Google.com/Docs: http://itunes.apple.com/us/app/godocs-for-google-docs/
id348792440?mt=8 or https://market.android.com/details?id=com.google.
android.apps.docs&hl=en

Google.com/Earth: http://itunes.apple.com/us/app/google-earth/
id293622097?mt=8 or https://market.android.com/details?id=com.google.
earth&hl=en

Google Goggles: http://www.google.com/mobile/goggles; https://market.
android.com/details?id=com.google.android.apps.unveil&hl=en

Google Presentations: http://www.google.com/google-d-s/presentations/

Google Talk: http://www.google.com/talk/

GoToMeeting.com

GoToWebinar: http://www.gotomeeting.com/fec/webinar

GoToMyPC.com

GotPrint.com or GotPrint.net

GrammarGirl: http://grammar.quickanddirtytips.com/

Groupon.com: http://itunes.apple.com/us/app/groupon/id352683833?mt=8 or
https://market.android.com/details?id=com.groupon&hl=en

Gubb.net

Guru.com

Highrisehq.com

HootSuite.com: http://itunes.apple.com/us/app/hootsuite-for-twitter/
id341249709?mt=8 or https://market.android.com/details?id=com.hootsuite.
droid.full&hl=en

HotelTonight.com: http://itunes.apple.com/us/app/hotel-tonight-last-minute/
id407690035?mt=8 or https://market.android.com/details?id=com.hoteltonight.
android.prod&hl=en

hulu.com: http://itunes.apple.com/us/app/hulu-plus/id376510438?mt=8 or
https://market.android.com/details?id=com.hulu.plus&hl=en

iBackup.com

iDress for Weather: http://itunes.apple.com/us/app/idress-for-weather/
id385227220?mt=8

InstantTeleseminar.com

Intuit Payment Network: https://ipn.intuit.com/

Intuit's GoPayment: http://gopayment.com/

iProRecorder.com: http://itunes.apple.com/us/app/iprorecorder-premier-voice/
id293842039?mt=8

iRecorder: http://itunes.apple.com/us/app/irecorder-pro-pocket-voice/
id285750155?mt=8

iTimeSheetLite: http://itunes.apple.com/us/app/itimesheetlite/
   id296280230?mt=8

Joomla.org

Keynote: http://itunes.apple.com/us/app/keynote/id361285480?mt=8

Klout.com

LinkedIn.com: http://itunes.apple.com/us/app/linkedin/id288429040?mt=8
   or https://market.android.com/details?id=com.linkedin.android&hl=en

LiveDrive.com: http://itunes.apple.com/us/app/livedrive-mobile/
   id338236137?mt=8 or https://market.android.com/details?id=com.
   livedrive&hl=en

Livingsocial.com: http://itunes.apple.com/us/app/livingsocial/
   id340295413?mt=8 or https://market.android.com/details?id=com.livingsocial.
   www&hl=en

Local.com

Lockerz Share: http://share.lockerz.com/

LogMeIn.com

MapsWithMe.com

MarketMeSuite.com

MediaFunnel.com

Meetup.com

MegaMeeting.com

Megareader.net: http://itunes.apple.com/us/app/megareader-2-million-free/
   id387136454?mt=8

Microsoft Office Live: http://www.microsoft.com/office/olsb/Splitter-EN-US.html

Mint.com: http://itunes.apple.com/us/app/mint.com-personal-finance/
   id300238550?mt=8 or https://market.android.com/details?id=com.
   mint&hl=en

Mobile.Conduit.com

MobileCoupons.com

MobiQpons: http://mobiqpons.en.softonic.com/iphone

ModularMerchant.com

Moodle.org

Mozy.com: http://itunes.apple.com/us/app/mozy/id427293902?mt=8 or
https://market.android.com/details?id=com.mozy.mobile.android&hl=en

MultiMeasures: http://itunes.apple.com/us/app/multimeasure/
id396067036?mt=8

MyBlogGuest.com

MyOtherDrive.com

MySpace.com: http://itunes.apple.com/us/app/myspace/id284792653?mt=8 or
https://market.android.com/details?id=com.myspace.android&hl=en

MyToolbox: http://itunes.apple.com/us/app/my-tool-box/id368371356?mt=8

Naymz.com

Ning.com

Note2Self: http://itunes.apple.com/us/app/note-2-self/id402785109?mt=12

ODesk.com

Office^2 HD: http://itunes.apple.com/us/app/office2-hd/id364361728?mt=8

OmniHotels.com: http://itunes.apple.com/us/app/omni-hotels/
id323991491?mt=8

OmniGraffle: http://itunes.apple.com/us/app/omnigraffle/id363225984?mt=8

ooVoo: http://itunes.apple.com/us/app/oovoo-video-chat/id428845974?mt=8 or
https://market.android.com/details?id=com.oovoo&hl=en

OpenPR.com

Packing (+TO DO): http://itunes.apple.com/us/app/packing-to-do!/
id294710480?mt=8

Pages: http://itunes.apple.com/us/app/pages/id361309726?mt=8

Paymate.com

Paypal.com: http://itunes.apple.com/us/app/paypal/id283646709?mt=8 or
https://market.android.com/details?id=com.paypal.android.p2pmobile&hl=en

PCAnywhere.com

PDF Converter: http://itunes.apple.com/us/app/pdf-converter-for-ipad/
id443795627?mt=8

PDF Presenter: http://itunes.apple.com/us/app/pdf-presenter-for-ipad/
id376809625?mt=8

PDF Reader: http://itunes.apple.com/us/app/pdf-reader-ipad-edition/
id367816156?mt=8

PDF-it: http://itunes.apple.com/us/app/pdf-it/id389982506?mt=8

PeerIndex.com

Photobucket.com: http://itunes.apple.com/us/app/photobucket/id314439840?mt=8 or https://market.android.com/details?id=com.photobucket.android&hl=en

PicasaWeb.Google.com

Ping.fm

PinpointSocial.com

Plaxo.com: http://itunes.apple.com/us/app/plaxo-address-book-backup/id377135604?mt=8

PodcastAlley.com

PodcastPickle.com

Point Inside Shopping & Travel: http://itunes.apple.com/us/app/point-inside-shopping-travel/id338171893?mt=8 or https://market.android.com/details?id=com.pointinside.android.app&hl=en

Portfolio Display: http://www.linkedin.com/opensocialInstallation/preview?_applicationId=104096&_ch_panel_id=1

PRLeap.com

PRLog.org

PRNewswire.com

PRWeb.com

Qontext.com: http://itunes.apple.com/us/app/qontext/id369873145?mt=8 or https://market.android.com/details?id=e2o.mobile&hl=en

Quickbooks.com

Quickoffice Pro HD: http://www.quickoffice.com/quickoffice_pro_hd_ipad/; http://itunes.apple.com/us/app/id376212724?mt=8; or https://market.android.com/details?id=com.qo.android.tablet.am&hl=en

QuickVoice2TextEmail: http://itunes.apple.com/us/app/quickvoice2text-email-pro/id285877935?mt=8

Quotationary.net: http://itunes.apple.com/us/app/quotationary/id306386514?mt=8

RadarScope: http://itunes.apple.com/us/app/radarscope/id288419283?mt=8 or https://market.android.com/details?id=com.basevelocity.radarscope

Refynr.com

RegOnline.com

RememberTheMilk.com: http://itunes.apple.com/us/app/remember-the-milk/
id293561396?mt=8 or https://market.android.com/details?id=com.
rememberthemilk.MobileRTM&hl=en

RogerEbert.SunTimescom: http://itunes.apple.com/us/app/
roger-eberts-great-movies/id421965337?mt=8

Saasmob.com

Say It & Mail It Pro Recorder: http://itunes.apple.com/us/app/
say-it-mail-it-pro-recorder/id363193938?mt=8

ShareThis.com

Shopper: http://itunes.apple.com/us/app/shopper-grocery-shopping-lists/
id284776127?mt=8

Sightspeed.com

SignUpGuy.com

SimpleMind+: http://itunes.apple.com/us/app/simplemind+-mind-mapping/
id305727658?mt=8

Simplenote: http://itunes.apple.com/us/app/simplenote/id289429962?mt=8

Skype.com: http://itunes.apple.com/us/app/skype/id304878510?mt=8 or
https://market.android.com/details?id=com.skype.raider&hl=en

SlideShare.net

Slideshark.com: http://itunes.apple.com/us/app/
slideshark-powerpoint-presentations/id471369684?mt=8

SocialOomph.com (formerly TweetLater)

SocialMention.com

Square: www.squareup.com; http://itunes.apple.com/us/app/square/
id335393788?mt=8 or https://market.android.com/details?id=com.
squareup&hl=en

StumbleUpon.com: http://itunes.apple.com/us/app/stumbleupon!/
id386244833?mt=8 or https://market.android.com/details?id=com.stumbleupon.
android.app&hl=en

SugarSync.com: http://itunes.apple.com/us/app/sugarsync/id288491637?mt=8
or https://market.android.com/details?id=com.sharpcast.sugarsync&hl=en

TalkFusion.com

TheWeatherChannel.com: http://itunes.apple.com/us/app/the-weather-channel/id295646461?mt=8 or https://market.android.com/details?id=com.weather.Weather&hl=en

TheWorldClock: http://itunes.apple.com/us/app/the-world-clock/id368177365?mt=8

Threadsy.com

Tickspot.com

TimeBridge.com

TimeLogger: http://itunes.apple.com/us/app/timelogger/id288769270?mt=8

Timely.is

TimeMaster + Billing: http://itunes.apple.com/us/app/time-master-+-billing/id310289408?mt=8

Timewerks: http://itunes.apple.com/us/app/timewerks-mobile-billing-pdf/id290385321?mt=8

TinyURL.com

Toggl.com: http://itunes.apple.com/us/app/toggl-timer/id330285564?mt=8 or https://market.android.com/details?id=com.toggl.timer

Triberr.com

TripAdvisor.com: http://itunes.apple.com/us/app/tripadvisor-hotels-flights/id284876795?mt=8 or https://market.android.com/details?id=com.tripadvisor.tripadvisor&hl=en

TripIt.com: http://itunes.apple.com/us/app/tripit-travel-organizer-free/id311035142?mt=8 or https://market.android.com/details?id=com.tripit&hl=en

Tungle.me: http://www.google.com/enterprise/marketplace/viewListing?productListingId=4626+18406874010889112579

TweetDeck.com: http://itunes.apple.com/us/app/tweetdeck/id429654148?mt=8 or https://market.android.com/details?id=com.thedeck.android.app&hl=en

uPackingList: http://itunes.apple.com/us/app/upackinglist/id323241118?mt=8 or https://market.android.com/details?id=com.nixsolutions.upack&hl=en

UPS Mobile: http://itunes.apple.com/us/app/ups-mobile/id336377331?mt=8 or https://market.android.com/details?id=com.ups.mobile.android&hl=en

UrbanSpoon.com: http://itunes.apple.com/us/app/urbanspoon/id284708449?mt=8 or https://market.android.com/details?id=com.urbanspoon&hl=en

USPS Mobile: http://itunes.apple.com/us/app/usps-mobile/id339597578?mt=8 or https://market.android.com/details?id=com.usps&hl=en

Vistaprint.com

Vonnage.com

Webex.com: http://itunes.apple.com/us/app/cisco-webex-meeting-center/id298844386?mt=8 or https://market.android.com/details?id=com.cisco.webex.meetings&hl=en

White Pages Mobile: http://itunes.apple.com/us/app/whitepages/id287734809?mt=8

Wi-FiFinder: http://itunes.apple.com/us/app/wi-fi-finder/id300708497?mt=8

Wiki.com

Wordpress.com

World Atlas HD: http://itunes.apple.com/us/app/world-atlas-hd/id364733950?mt=8

WorldCard Mobile: http://itunes.apple.com/us/app/worldcard-mobile-business/id333211045?mt=8 or https://market.android.com/details?id=com.penpower.bcr.worldcard

WorldExplorer: http://itunes.apple.com/us/app/world-explorer/id381581095?mt=8

WriteRoom: http://itunes.apple.com/us/app/writeroom/id288751446?mt=8

Yahoo.com: http://itunes.apple.com/us/app/yahoo!/id304158842?mt=8

Yelp.com: http://itunes.apple.com/us/app/yelp/id284910350?mt=8 or https://market.android.com/details?id=com.yelp.android&hl=en

YouNote: http://itunes.apple.com/us/app/younote!/id284969305?mt=8

YouSendIt.com

YouTube.com (included on iPad): https://market.android.com/details?id=com.google.android.youtube&hl=en

YPMobile: http://itunes.apple.com/us/app/yp-local-search-gas-prices/
   id284806204?mt=8

Yugma.com

Yuuguu.com

Zagat.com: http://itunes.apple.com/us/app/zagat/id296428490?mt=8 or
   https://market.android.com/details?id=com.semaphoremobile.zagat.android

Zoho Planner: www.planner.zoho.com

Zoolit.com

Index

About the Author

Gail Z. Martin is an author, entrepreneur, and international speaker on marketing for small business and solo professionals. She owns DreamSpinner Communications, helping companies create better marketing results in just 30 days. She works with companies, coaches, consultants, authors, speakers, and nonprofits throughout North America. Martin holds an MBA in marketing from The Pennsylvania State University, and has more than 25 years of marketing experience, including corporate and nonprofit senior executive roles. She founded DreamSpinner Communications in 2004.

Gail speaks to international audiences on social media, small business marketing, book promotion, and defining success. Whether it's a keynote presentation, workshop, seminar, or breakout session, Martin's high-energy, down-to-earth style energizes and provides a clear road to action.

Gail extends the strategies from her books through group and one-on-one coaching programs, teleseminars, custom consulting, e-books, and home study programs. Learn more at www. GailMartinMarketing.com.

In addition to this book, Gail is also the author of *30 Days to Online PR and Marketing Success: The 30 Day Results Guide to Making the Most of Online Promotion to Grab Headlines and Get Clients* and *30 Days to Social Media Success: The 30 Day Results Guide to Making the Most of Twitter, Blogging, LinkedIn, and Facebook,* as well as *The Thrifty Author's Guide* series, which providers her unique approach to book marketing (*www.ThriftyAuthor.com*).

Gail Martin is the host of the Shared Dreams Marketing Podcast, where she interviews thought leaders, trendsetters, and notable entrepreneurs and authors (*www.SharedDreamsPodcast.com*). She's on Facebook as Gail Martin, 30 Day Results Guide, and The Thrifty Author, and on Twitter @GailMartinPR. Gail is the co-host of the Big Dreams and Hard Work blog, sharing insights into social media and online marketing for small business. (*www.BigDreamsAndHardWork.com*)

Gail is also the author of the bestselling fantasy adventure series, *The Chronicles of the Necromancer* (*The Summoner, The Blood King, Dark Haven, Dark Lady's Chosen*) from Solaris Books, and *The Fallen Kings Cycle* (*The Sworn, The Dread*) and the new *Ascendant Kingdoms Saga* from Orbit Books. Find her fiction online at www.ChroniclesOfTheNecromancer.com.

Gail Martin lives in Charlotte, North Carolina with her family.

Contact Gail Z. Martin online at Gail@GailMartinMarketing.com.